PREACHING THE CHRISTMAS STORY

PREACHING THE CHRISTMAS STORY

Hugh Litchfield

BROADMAN PRESS
Nashville, Tennessee

© Copyright 1984 • Broadman Press
All Rights reserved.
4221-01
ISBN: 0-8054-2101-7
Dewey Decimal Classification: 252.61
Subject Heading: CHRISTMAS—SERMONS
Library of Congress Catalog Number: 83-071689
Printed in the United States of America
Unless otherwise indicated, all Scripture quotations are from the Revised
Standard Version of the Bible, copyrighted 1946, 1952, © 1971, 1973.

Library of Congress Cataloging in Publication Data

Litchfield, Hugh, 1940-
  Preaching the Christmas story.

  1. Christmas sermons. 2. Baptists—Sermons.
3. Sermons, American.   I. Title.
BV4257.L57 1984   252'.061   83-71689
ISBN 0-8054-2101-7

To Sarah

Who helps my story come alive.

Preface

Christmas is a tremendous time in the celebration of our faith. It reminds us of the love of God that was so strong that it was willing to come into the world where we were to try to find and save us. God came to be with us! What a glorious truth!

Christmas is a time for joy, singing, family gatherings, presents, and pretty-colored trees. But most of all, Christmas is a time for worship: once again, we offer ourselves to this One who loves us so. We cannot really celebrate Christmas without worship.

That involves preaching the Christmas story. That is both a challenge and a joy. It is a challenge to try to bring the familiar story to life again, but a joy to see what happens when it reaches out and lives again in the lives of the people.

What I have presented in this book is a result of my years of struggling with both the challenge and the joy of preaching the Christmas story. I hope that what I have discovered may be helpful to you in discovering Christmas anew.

There are a few matters I need to take care of at the beginning. All of the quotations of Scripture used in this book are from the Revised Standard Version unless otherwise indicated. A deep expression of thanksgiving is given to Muriel Hoggard who has typed and retyped this material. The work could not have been done without her perseverance.

Special thanks are given to the kind and gracious people of Azalea Baptist Church in Norfolk, Virginia, for their encouragement and support. They have made preaching the Christmas story an exciting and rewarding experience.

Contents

Introduction

An experienced preacher friend shocked me one day by asking, "Can you give me some advice on how to preach about Christmas? I find this the hardest time to preach during the year. I just can't seem to get enough ideas."

I could hardly believe my ears. My experience had been just the opposite. I enjoyed preaching at Christmas more than any other time of the year. All the celebration, music, and excitement seemed to spur me on to the task.

After all, Christmas is one of the major Christian holy days. It is so full of meaning. How could anyone have trouble preaching about Christmas?

But my friend had a point. He had been at his church for over ten years. He had tried to explain the story of Christmas in every way he knew how, but he seemed to have exhausted its meaning.

What could he do to keep the Christmas story alive? How could he present it in a way that would catch the excitement of it anew for his people? Was there any advice I could give to help him in the task?

It is always presumptuous to try to give advice to anyone on how they should preach. How I do it may not be the right way for someone else. However, the question has haunted me ever since I heard it. Was there any advice I could have given to help preach the Christmas story? And it is a *story*.

The movement in homiletical circles today is emphasis on preaching as "telling the story." The Bible is the story of how God worked in human history to bring salvation to people. It is a story full of drama and action, centering on real live flesh and blood persons.

The task for preaching is to tell God's story to the people in such a way that it becomes *their* story. They will listen and see themselves in it, what part they play, and hopefully discover their great need of Christ for life and for hope.

Is there a way we can tell the Christmas story so this will happen? How can the Christmas story come alive and become part of the story of those who sit in the pews?

For me, the key to preaching at Christmas is to preach it as a series. Instead of trying to speak on a different subject every Sunday, I try to develop one major theme for the Christmas season and plan every sermon around that theme.

The exciting challenge is to attempt to discover some theme, some approach to the Christmas story that will catch its meaning and help it live among the people. I have done this for the past several years and have been pleased with the results. I have found several advantages in preaching Christmas in a series.

Advantages of Series Preaching

Heightens interest

To preach Christmas as a series heightens the interest of the hearer. They have a chance to see the Christmas story as a story, with all of the parts fitting together. With one central theme around which to organize their Christmas worship, they can make better sense of it.

Each year, our church staff sends out a pamphlet to all the members with the subjects and activities of the Christmas season outlined around the specific theme to be used. With this worship guide, the people will be able to understand the parts of the puzzle that we will try to put together for them. Each Sunday will be important for it will add a new part to the understanding of the Christmas story.

To see that the Christmas season makes sense, that it is not just a hodgepodge of activities and ideas, will bring more interest in your preaching. I always feel gratified when, as we near the Christmas season, people begin to ask, "What is going to be the theme of Christmas this year?" That reflects Christmas preaching that has remained interesting.

Keeps preaching balanced

One of the problems of our preaching is that it can become too unbalanced. We preach on one theme or doctrine more than we do another. We ride our own favorite subject or "hobbyhorse" until our people are tired of it.

It is important to preach the sinfulness of people, but it is also important to preach the grandeur of humanity in the eyes of God. It is all right to preach about grace, but we also need to preach law. We must touch upon all the major themes of the Bible and of the Christmas faith.

Having a specific theme at Christmas can help us keep balance in our preaching. To prepare a series on the Christmas story should cause us to wrestle with the main doctrines and ideas of the Bible.

The Christmas story is about God's tremendous love for people, but it is also about the sinfulness of people which made Christmas a necessity. We can talk about the great hope that Christ came to dwell with us, but we can also point out the realistic fact of suffering as Herod slaughtered innocent children.

The Christmas story is a microcosm of the Christian faith. Preaching the story of Christmas will give the chance to deal with ideas and subjects that we may have neglected during the year. Developing a series to deal with Christmas can help our preaching become more balanced.

Enhances relevance

We want our people to understand that the Bible is talking about them. We want them to understand that the Word of God is a living word and they are involved in it. When they hear the Bible story, we hope they will see themselves in it and understand that what is being said is for them. I feel that preaching the story of Christmas will do that when it is organized around one central theme. People will understand it better; and, when they do that, they will be able to apply it easier to their own lives.

To do this, we must see the Scripture about Christmas as a story. It is just that. It is so full of drama and action. A young girl discovers she is to bear the Christ child: the cruel situation of a long journey for the purpose of taxation; no room in the inn; a stable manger becomes the cradle for the baby; shepherds and Wise Men and a star overhead; Herod's jealous insecurity prompts a quick night flight to Egypt!

The Christmas story is high drama. It is an exciting story that can capture the imagination and interest of almost everyone.

Preaching that is alive puts the people into the story. They become Joseph, trying to provide a place for the birth of the child. They become the shepherds who marvel at the angel's announcement of the new birth. They become the Wise Men who offer their gifts to this newborn King. They even become Herod, full of fear and anxiety, who seeks to eliminate this baby.

Preaching the Christmas story as a story organized carefully around a special theme can help it come alive to the hearers. They become more than hearers; they become the participants in the story themselves. The word becomes relevant. The Christmas story can become their story.

Helps in planning the whole celebration of Christmas at the church

The worship of Christmas does not just involve preaching. It involves music and parties and other kinds of celebrations. To have a central theme for Christmas should make it easier to plan the total Christmas celebration of the church.

Music in the worship service and music specials can be coordinated around the one central theme. Theme Christmas parties can be held in the church. Special dramatic presentations could be done on the theme. Organizing Christmas around a central theme or series can open up a whole realm of possibilities for the church's celebration of Christmas.

Makes the Christmas story exciting to the preacher

One of the main benefits for me in preaching a series at Christmas has been to keep the Christmas story alive. It does not seem to be a familiar story that I've read so many times. Instead, in seeking to discover the many ways to approach the Christmas Scripture, it has stayed alive and exciting for me. It is not old hat but an unending gold mine of treasures unlimited.

Trying to organize the story around a simple theme forces me to rethink the story, to wrestle with its many meanings and movements. To do that is to become involved with the story itself, to have it grip me all over again. It becomes my story! When that happens to me, I become so excited about it that I just can't wait to share with my people what I have discovered. When the Scripture stays alive for me, it will come alive for my people.

These advantages are well worth the attempt to preach from a series at Christmas. If Christmas has become a curse to you and not a blessing, try to develop some series theme that will put the sense of it together for you.

There are many themes covered in the Christmas story to help you begin. Christmas is so valuable because it does deal with the major themes of the Christian faith. I think we need to keep these themes in mind as we seek to prepare our Christmas series.

Themes of Christmas Preaching

The love of God

The Christmas story echoes the major theme of the Bible, that of

God's great love for his people. Christmas happened because God would not give up on them. He had every reason to forsake them. They had rebelled against him more times than they could remember. They deserved to be forgotten. But God did not forget! He came to those who had rejected him and who would reject him again. He came to bring forgiveness and hope to them. Love was the reason he came: love—unconditional, unending, undeserved! That's why the angels sang at Christmas. "God so loved the world" that he came to live in it and "pitch his tent" with his people.

This is a never-ending theme that we still need to preach over and over again. Just as God came to Bethlehem because of his great love for his children, so he still comes in Christ to us to love us still. We are undeserving of that love, but it does not matter. He comes anyway to offer us hope and forgiveness. What good news! What a Christmas story! It was true then, and it is true now! What exciting news to preach!

The Doctrine of Sin

The background of the Christmas story provides an excellent opportunity to develop the doctrine of sin. Christmas happened because of God's response to human sinfulness. People had rebelled against God and his will, tried to live by their own wisdom. They had not succeeded. They kept getting deeper and deeper into trouble, a trouble from which they could not escape.

Meant to be a people who blessed all the nations of the world, Israel had become a scattered and captive nation. Their oppression under the Romans was a consequence of their rebellion against God. Christmas offers the chance to look at sin and all of its terrible consequences. From having to register to be taxed to Herod's insecurity which caused him to seek the death of a tiny baby boy, the deadly results of sin can be seen. The fallen condition of humanity can be preached at Christmas very easily.

The Doctrine of Redemption

Christmas rings with the good news that the baby will be called Jesus because "he will save his people from their sins" (Matt. 1:21). Salvation has come in Christ! What does that mean? How could God undo what mankind had done? How did his coming deal with the fact of sin? What did God do to reunite himself with humanity?

These questions can be answered through the Christmas story. Christ's coming was a major chapter in the history of salvation. His coming led him to a cross. We must not leave Christ in the manger! His love which leads to forgiveness needs to be proclaimed anew. The breaking down of the barrier of sin needs to be highlighted. Christmas was the beginning of the end for all that would separate human beings from God. Salvation has come, and it is available to anyone who needs it. That is a word for all people at all times.

The Theme of Hope

One of the most desperate questions of people is, "Is there any hope?" In the face of never-ending problems, we wonder if there is any way out of them. Solutions seem few and far between. Such was the situation for the Jewish people when that first Christmas occurred. They were desperately looking for hope. They were an oppressed people, and they hoped it would end. They were suffering, and they hoped it would stop. They were waiting for God's Messiah, and they hoped he would come. They were caught in misery and unhappiness, and they hoped for a way out. Was there any hope for them?

Christmas was a definite word of hope for them. In the coming of Christ was all the hope they needed. It was not a hope that was akin to whistling in the dark. It was a realistic hope that would be based on what Christ was and on what he did. He would bring them freedom of spirit. He would deliver them from their bondage to sin. He would show them the way to joy and to happiness. Christmas told them that Christ was their hope and if they trusted him he would lead them into the kingdom that would last forever.

We have the same answer today. Where is our hope? It is not in persons, programs, or material things. It still lies in the power of Christ who will lead us into his kingdom that will be forever. We need hope to live. Christmas brings that hope, and we can announce it again.

The Theme of Joy

"Joy to the world! The Lord is come." So the angels sang. The people needed some joy, for they had their share of sorrow and bad times. But the secret of joy was in the truth that Jesus had come to be with them, to help them and to stand with them as they made their way through life. That was true joy, the confidence of God's presence with them.

This is a word we need to preach today. We are a generation that will try anything to make us happy. But what we try does not bring happiness if it does not include trusting Christ. True joy comes from the confidence we can have in knowing that he is with us in the midst of all of life. No matter what happens to us, we do not have to face it alone. Christ is there with us. That is the source of joy. Joy comes from inside, not from external circumstances or things. Christmas provides an opportunity to distinguish between true joy and false worldly happiness. This theme can be sounded: "Joy to the world! the Lord is come."

The Question of Suffering

The Christmas story takes in all the realities of life, good and bad. Part of the Christmas story has to do with the question of suffering. Suffering is a harsh part of life, but it must be faced. In those days, the very people of God were under captivity and were struggling hard just to survive.

Why was survival so hard? Herod's soldiers brought suffering and sorrow to many parents as their children were murdered. Why did the innocent have to suffer? The newborn baby was taken down into Egypt in order to escape death. Why did God allow that to happen?

All the searching questions are there in the Christmas story. The shadow of a cross surrounded the whole story, a cross of suffering and death. We cannot separate the cross from the Christmas story. We can not run away from the hard questions about suffering.

Christmas does not give us all the final answers about the problem, but it does provide some hints and clues as to how it may be faced. As we preach at Christmas, we must not avoid the dark side of life. People know what it is like and we must help them to understand and face it.

The Nature of God

Christmas provides some interesting insights into the very nature and character of God. The basic insight is that God can not be captured by human thoughts and schemes.

The religious people of that day thought they had God all figured out. They knew what would happen when the Messiah came. He would come in spectacular ways to overthrow the Roman oppressors All would be convinced of his mighty power. They would tremble at his coming.

But it didn't happen that way. He did not come as a mighty warrior but as a tiny, helpless baby. There were no heavenly trumpets announcing his coming to all the world: just some angels telling it to a few shepherds and a star for Wise Men to follow.

There was no palace for him, just a manger in the back of some inn in Bethlehem. As a result, those religious leaders could not recognize God even when he was among them. They were not open to his unpredictability.

God is just like that: full of surprises. We can't pin him down into one set of beliefs or into one kind of creed. God is so surprising! He loves those no one else cares about. He goes where no one else would think God would go—all the way to a cross of crucifixion. He forgives even his enemies. He welcomes into the kingdom harlots and tax collectors and all sorts of riffraff. He comforts the afflicted and afflicts the comfortable. He is God and there is no one to compare with him.

Christmas is that opportunity to see him again in this light, to once again remember that we must not try to capture God in our human terms only. He is greater than that. We must be always open to the truth that God can come to us in new ways, in unexpected events, in surprising moments. Christmas is the time to remember how great God really is!

The Way of Discipleship

The Christmas story provides several examples of what it means to be a follower of Christ. The two basic qualities of discipleship are trust and obedience, and there were those who showed these qualities. Mary was one. She was chosen to be the mother of the baby. She did not understand it all, but she was a believer in God and trusted him to know what was best. She obeyed and did what was asked. Joseph was another who trusted and obeyed. It was very hard for him to make sense out of what had happened. When the angel appeared to him and told him the meaning of it, he was a faithful servant from that moment on. He provided carefully for the needs of Mary. The Wise Men came and bowed before the newborn king. Their wisdom did not prevent them from humbly worshiping the Christ. They gave him expensive gifts, a sign of their devotion. The shepherds came and saw the baby and then went out to tell others what they had seen. They became witnesses for Christ.

The basic elements of discipleship are contained in the story. Trust, obedience, worship, giving, witnessing—these are the deeds we must do for Christ today. The response to the discovery of Christ should be a willingness to serve him. Christmas preaching can emphasize that.

The Discovery of Meaning

One of the frustrations of those who were living during that first Christmas was that they did not understand the meaning of their existence. They saw no "rhyme or reason" to what was happening. They had trusted in God, but it seemed as if he had forgotten them. They struggled hard just to survive, but they were wondering why. There was so much senseless suffering that they hated. What was the purpose of it all? It seemed that there was no meaning in life whatsoever.

Christ's coming brought meaning and purpose back into life. They began to understand that God was still in control of life. He had not abandoned them. They were still his people and he would continue to work out his purposes among them. He had not been defeated by the Romans or by anything else. If they held on to him, he would help them live and come through all their difficulties. His coming reaffirmed their hope that the kingdom of God was coming, that nothing could prevent it. To be in his kingdom and to serve him was the goal and purpose of life. Christmas brought meaning back into life for them.

This is a message modern people need to hear. Life often seems meaningless. Far too many are struggling to make it through the day, with no earthly reason why. The high rate of suicides, especially among the young, is a testimony to the loss of meaning in the lives of people. Too many feel that life is going nowhere and that existence is a bore.

Christmas gives the opportunity to reevaluate that idea. Christ's coming into the world brought new meaning for us. He is God with us, a God who seeks to help us live, but also a God who is still working his purposes out among us. Since Christmas happened, we know that love is still the way to live, justice and righteousness are not a waste of time, and one day the lion will lie down by the lamb (see Isa. 11:6-9). The kingdom of God will be established, and all that is done for it will not be in vain. The purpose of life is to serve this Christ who is with us. If we faithfully do that, life will take on new meaning and purpose. To give our lives away to him will bring new life to us, now and forevermore.

These are just a few of the mighty themes that Christmas presents. These themes alone will provide a wealth of preaching material. Christmas is about the way to life and to preach *that* is what people desperately need to hear.

What follows is my attempt to try to do just that. The sermon series are examples of some of my attempts to apply the themes of Christmas to the lives of people. Through these sermons, I have basically touched upon all of the themes I have presented here. They are not exhaustive. Hopefully, you will be inspired to devise ways to preach on other themes. That can be done. The Christmas story provides "potential unlimited" for the preaching of the gospel. With the use of an imagination that seeks to immerse itself in the story, many truths will come alive for you.

Christmas is an exciting time to preach. God came in Christ into the manger in Bethlehem. The glory of it all is that God still comes into the lives of people in our churches through the sermons we preach about his coming. What a joy it is to preach that wonderful Christmas message, "Emmanuel, God with us" (see Matt. 1:23).

Series One
Christmas Personalities

One of the easiest ways to preach the Christmas story is through the people who were involved in it. The list is quite long. For this series, I chose several persons who were central in the action of that first Christmas. Their lives revealed the significance and meaning of the coming of Christ.

Sermons

Joseph: Being Ready for Christmas
Herod: The Curse of Christmas
The Wise Men: Being Caught by a Vision
Mary and Joseph: Carrying Christmas into Life

Being Ready for Christmas

(Matt. 1:18-25)

Let me ask you a question: Are you ready for Christmas? You're probably saying, "What a stupid question. This is just the first week of December. Who's ready for Christmas? We've got a lot of things to do. All the cards to send out, the presents to buy and wrap, the houses to decorate, the trees to put up. Ready for Christmas? You've got to be kidding."

I can understand what you mean because I'm not ready for Christmas, either. One of my protests against the commercialization of Christmas is a resolve not to do anything to get ready for Christmas until after Thanksgiving. Ready for Christmas? Heavens, no!

Usually when we talk about getting ready for Christmas, we talk about deeds we have to do. However, I'm not talking about deeds, I'm talking about attitude. This is the most important part of our Christmas celebration anyway. What is our approach to the Christmas season? What is our attitude toward it? You hear people say, "I just can't seem to get into the Christmas spirit this year." They're talking about attitude, one's approach to what Christmas is all about. When I want us to be ready for Christmas, I want us to have that kind of openness this Christmas to the coming and doing of God in our lives.

This is what Christmas is all about. It's the celebration of God breaking into the arena of human life, pitching his tent with us, walking with us, being with us. Since that is true, we ought to be living on tiptoes, ready for the coming of God at any time, at any place, in any way. Is this the way we're approaching Christmas, with that kind of openness?

Enter Joseph, an often neglected member of the Christmas story but one who played a most vital part. Here was a man who lived with an openness to God. If he hadn't been open and committed to God, then

Joseph would have been a very insignificant part of our Christmas story and the whole story would have been changed.

But because of Joseph's approach to the Christmas event, he was ready for Christmas. How do we know he was ready for Christmas? What is it that we have to do and be in order to have the right attitude toward Christmas?

1. To be ready for Christmas we need to trust God, confident that he knows what he's doing.

Joseph was a man of faith, but he was not a man whose faith was always easy. There were those moments when it was difficult for him. Imagine the situation. He was in love with Mary, anticipating the day when he would be married to her. Then she hit him with a bombshell: "I'm going to have a baby." He didn't understand it. It broke his heart. He was sure she had been unfaithful to him. The law said such a person should be stoned to death, but Joseph loved Mary too much to allow that to happen.

While he was considering what to do, God spoke to him in a dream. He told Joseph, "Don't worry about it. I'm in this thing. The child that's going to be born is one who will grow up to save the people from their sins. I'm in it, trust me with it. Take Mary for your wife and look after her."

I'm sure Joseph had a lot of questions he wanted to ask about the situation. But in spite of that, the story tells us that Joseph took Mary for his wife and did what God told him to do. He was someone who didn't understand all that was going on, but he did understand one thing: God could be trusted. In the midst of all of it, he would at least trust him to know what he was doing. Since he did, Christmas happened.

Now we are people of faith, but at times it gets difficult to keep. As we look at all that's going on in the world, and as we look at what happens in our own personal lives, it gets hard to hold on to God. We talk about peace, but we live in the midst of a world torn by war. Where's God in all of that? We know that people still die by the thousands each day of hunger. We know that there is still poverty and illiteracy all across the face of this globe. We know that inflation eats away at our pocketbooks and makes it a struggle for many just to survive. Cancer and leukemia, heart disease and emphysema—they are diseases that are still with us and we wish they weren't. Where is God in the midst of all of that?

There are those that laugh at any thought that God might be in this world, much less in control of it. How can you talk of love in the face of so much hate? How can you talk of good in the face of so much bad? How can you talk of peace in the face of so much war? How can you praise God in the light of so much suffering?

Does God know what he is doing? We might wonder about that. Despair and hopelessness can creep into our spirits. Then Christmas comes! Christmas reminds us that God can be trusted, for in those days there was darkness over the face of the earth, too. There was heartbreak and misery and suffering and pain. It seemed as if God was far away, but he wasn't. Instead, God was right there in the middle of them and into that darkness, the flicker of a little light spread into a tremendous flame. God was there.

At times, that is hard to see. One of our problems is that we look for God in different ways and in the wrong places. H. G. Wells was a man who thought of greatness in terms of big buildings and lots of people. He was criticizing a small humanitarian society because they were so small and what they were able to do seemed to be so little. He said, "Go into London and look at the big buildings and the magnificent palaces of business. Look at all of the traffic jams and the multitudes of people. Look at all of that and tell me what can you accomplish in the face of it."

Someone said, "If H. G. Wells had been living 2,000 years ago, he may have been coming down the road one day from Jerusalem to Jericho and run into a group of footsore fishermen and what nots, rag-tags, making their way up to the Holy City. H. G. Wells would have taken Jesus over to the side and said, 'What in the world are you trying to do, you with all of these fishermen and all of these rag-tag people? Go up to Jerusalem and here's what I want you to do. Take a big look at all the Roman soldiers and all of their might. Go up to the temple and look at the chief rabbi. See all the Romans and Israelites busily involved in business at work, very content with the way things are. Look at all of it and tell me, what in the world can you do to change any of that? You can't do a thing.'"[1]

What can a baby boy born in some out-of-the-way stable do? Nothing, but grow up and change the world, that's all, because God was in it. In our darkness, Christmas causes us to remember that God is still with us and that he is still at work in this world. We can trust him. He has not forsaken us. We can live this Christmas with a sense of openness because we can see it—if we have the eyes to see it—love and joy and peace and life because God is here! He is here now! He is here with you now! We can trust him!

2. To be ready for Christmas, we need to be carers of others.

The main part that Joseph seemed to have played in the Christmas story was to take care of Mary. He was sensitive to her every need. He surrounded her with a sense of security and love, shielded her from some of the ridicule and gossip that surely came their way. He helped provide a place for her to have the baby, staying with her through that dark night and comforting her in the midst of the pain. Joseph's part in the Christmas story was to care for Mary, to minister to her every need, and that Joseph did. Since Joseph cared, Christmas happened.

Christmas is the time where it seems that we do reach out to care for others in special ways. We have many good causes at Christmas: the Joy Fund that seeks to provide toys for needy children; food baskets for the hungry; presents for prisoners behind bars; gifts for lonely people in nursing homes; and so much more. All this is good.

Of course, caring for others and for their needs ought to be a yearlong way of life. Christmas tells us about a God who cared so much for us that he was willing to come down, even at the risk of his life, to minister to us. Christmas calls us to the same kind of doing, the same kind of caring.

The needs are all around us. The hungry are here, thousands each day, dying for lack of food. I won't forget the front page of a *Time* magazine. It had a picture of a starving Cambodian baby: the swollen stomach; the shriveled body; the big eyes bulging from the head. It's a picture I won't easily forget. The sad thing about it is that there are so many people just like that, dying because they don't have food to eat. Does it move us? Does it move us enough to miss a meal a week and take the money that we would have paid for that meal and use it to help feed the hungry?

There are in Norfolk 1,500 runaway teenagers each year. They run for various reasons. They can't stand home any more, they want to be free, they are abused. These children are confused, bewildered, and sometimes battered. They need people to care for them. Do we care enough to provide foster homes or big brothers and big sisters to care for them?

The lonely people who dwell in the nursing homes, the lonely people who move into our neighborhoods from other places, looking for someone to say, "Hi." Do we? There is human need at our doorsteps and, for Christmas to be what it ought to be, we have to care for other people.

As the Christmas story tells us, caring for other people is a way of serving God.

There was a Czechoslovakian film called *Adrift.* It was about a fisherman and his family who one day rescued a girl from drowning. The girl came to live with him for a while. He couldn't find anything about her past. It was a mystery. In those years that the little girl lived with them, she was a source of untold blessings and untold joy, binding that family together in love.

Near the end of the film, the girl disappeared just as mysteriously as she had appeared. He looked for her and three other men came to try to help him in the search. Only when they revealed their identity did he begin to understand: Balthasar, Melchior, Gaspar—the supposed names of the Wise Men. What the fisherman began to understand was that in ministering to the needs of that little girl, he had cared for the very presence of God. In doing that he had come alive.[2]

The most alive people I know are those who have gotten themselves off their hands and are ministering and caring for others. To be ready for Christmas is to be ready to care, to minister, to reach out to touch the lives of someone else for God's sake. Are we ready for that?

3. To be ready for Christmas, we need to be givers to God of all that we are.

I wonder if anybody told Joseph how dangerous it would be to serve as the earthly father of Christ? Right after the birth of Baby Jesus, he had to take Mary and the baby and run for his life into the land of Egypt because of Herod. The king was insecure and jealous and sought to do away with this baby he felt would be a threat to his throne.

He began searching for him, killing babies two years of age and under. Joseph had to run for his life. It was dangerous. Would Joseph be willing to risk his life? Would Joseph be willing to do all that God asked? Joseph was. Whatever God needed him to do, he was willing to do.

Has anybody ever told us that there is a cost involved in being a Christian? There is! There will be those in this world who will not like those of us who are Christians. There are values in this world that stand against everything we value as Christians. We might lose some popularity if we stand up for what we believe is right and best and just. It will cost us time as we immerse ourselves in the ministries of Christ. It will cost money as we support the ministries of Christ with our finances. It might cost us our lives, as we stand up to fight against prejudice, the rise of racist organizations, injustice and wrong.

Are we willing to give God everything he needs from us in order to see that his will be done? Christmas is not as meaningful to many because they cannot say to God, "Whatever you want, I'll give; wherever you lead, I'll go; whatever you ask, I'll do." To be ready for Christmas, we can offer to God no less than everything he wants.

One of my favorite Christmas stories was told by Dina Donahue in *Guideposts* magazine. It was about a nine-year-old boy named Wally Purling. Wally was big for his age and was also a little slow mentally. But although big, he wasn't a bully. Everybody liked him. He was nice to all the little kids; in fact, he took up for them all the time.

They were doing a Christmas program in his school and Wally wanted to be in it. He wanted to be a shepherd, but the teacher had another part in mind for him. She wanted him to be the innkeeper because he was so big. Wally took the part home and studied it and practiced it hard.

The night came for the play, and everything was going smoothly. It came to the time when Mary and Joseph knocked on the door of the inn and Wally opened the door and said, "What do you want?" Joseph said, "We need a place to stay for the night." "You've got to find it somewhere else; the inn is full." "Are you sure?" Joseph asked. "We've come a long way, and it's cold." "No. There's no place here, go someplace else." "But my wife is going to have a baby, isn't there some corner we can hide in?"

At this point in the play there was silence, one of those embarrassing silences that made you believe that somebody had forgotten his line. Wally stood there, not saying anything. The prompter whispered, "No, be gone!" So Wally said, "No, be gone!" Joseph put his arm around Mary and turned to walk away from the inn.

It was at this point that this Christmas play took an unusual twist. Wally was big, but he had a heart just as big and he couldn't stand seeing Mary and Joseph walk away. He suddenly said, "Wait a minute, Joseph. Bring Mary on back. You can have my room. I'll sleep in the cold."[3]

There were those who said that the Christmas story was ruined, but I think not. In that little event was caught the whole essence of it: a boy willing to sleep out in the cold so that Mary and Joseph could have what they needed for the coming of the Christ child. Maybe we would enjoy Christmas a whole lot more if we were willing to sleep out in the cold for Christ, if we had to.

There are a lot of activities that you and I have to do to be ready for

Christmas. But while there are a lot of things I have to do, I hope that I'm ready for Christmas. I hope that in my attitude I am living on tiptoe, looking in every place and in every experience for the coming of God in a new and special way, for God is with us.

As we trust him and care for others, as we come to the place where we are willing to give ourselves to him, he can come in new and special ways.

NOTES

1. Halford Luccock, *A Sprig of Holly* (New York: The Pilgrim Press, 1978), pp. 52-53.

2. Haymon Scott, "What Are You Waiting For?" Unpublished sermon: First Presbyterian Church, Stamford, Connecticut, Jan. 1980, pp. 3-4.

3. James Flamming, "Christmas Is Always New," *Proclaim,* (Oct.-Dec. 1976), p. 39.

The Curse of Christmas

(Matt. 2:13-19)

There are those for whom Christmas is an unwelcome time, to whom Christmas is a curse and not a celebration. Did you know that crimes of murder and violence rise during the Christmas season? Suicides are higher during the Christmas season than any other time of the year. Psychiatric treatment and entrance into psychiatric hospitals rise during the Christmas season.

A survey was taken asking people, "Do you look forward to the Christmas season?" A few said yes, but by far the great majority of them said no and they seemed to indicate that they looked forward to the Christmas season with a sense of dread.[1] It has caused someone to rewrite one of the Christmas carols to say: "O little town of tension,/how jittery we see thee lie./Above thy deep and dreamless sleep/our shooting fears go by./Yet, in thy dark street shineth/the everlasting fright./The hopes and fears of all the years/shall visit us tonight."[2]

Fear and fright, suicide and depression, hopelessness and despair—that is the Christmas spirit for far too many. They do not want it. They wish it were gone. Christmas for them is a curse.

Why has Christmas become a curse for so many? There are many reasons. Christmas has become a curse for many because it reminds them of what they ought to be but are not. Christmas is a time of joy, and they have not really known it. Christmas is a time of love, and they have not really experienced it. Christmas is a time of goodwill to men, and they don't want to give it. Christmas is a time of hope, but they feel so hopeless and helpless. For many, Christmas is a reminder of what they could be, but are not. To be faced with your shortcomings, with the fact that you are not what you ought to be, is very discomforting.

There are many that don't want to wrestle with the fact that they are not what they ought to be. Christmas to them is a curse. For Christ demands the choice. Will we be what he wants us to be or not? One of the Christmas personalities was a man named Herod. He was a king and was one person we wish we could erase from the Christmas story. But we can't. He's there in the middle of it, with all of his terror. So frightened was he of Christ that he tried to get rid of him. How could he do that? How could he go out and send his soldiers to kill baby boys two years and under? How could he do that horrible deed? Why had Christmas become such a curse to him that he had become a curse to it?

Why is it that we don't always get out of Christmas what we should?

1. Christmas can become a curse whenever we push God out of our understanding of who we are.

Herod didn't know who he was. You could tell that by what frightened him. He was the king—mighty and powerful. What was he afraid of? A tiny, helpless baby boy, born to parents of poverty. It's quite a laugh to see a mighty king tremble and shudder at the thought of a tiny baby boy. But this is what Herod did.

Herod had no confidence in himself. He was not at peace with himself. He didn't know who he was because he hadn't taken God into account in his life. When Herod went about determining who he was and what his value was, he determined it by the world's standards. The world said you were somebody if you had a lot of power, a lot of money, a lot of prestige and position. Herod had all of that. In the eyes of the world, he was somebody. But inside, he was not at peace. Inside, he was full of turmoil and insecurity and anxiety because he had not come to accept himself as a child of God. He was defining himself by what others thought and as long as he did that he would never be at peace.

I am afraid that too many are going through life defining themselves by what the world says is important. We want to be somebody, so what do we have to do? We need to be successful and that means having power, prestige or wealth. So we compete with one another. We define ourselves by what others are. We've got to be the richest, the most popular, the most successful. We compete with one another and whenever somebody does better than we do we feel threatened, insecure, inadequate. Something's the matter with us because others seem to be better. We have defined ourselves by the wrong standards.

Gary Moore was awarded by CBS for all those years of television by being made a vice-president of the network. One of his friends was saying that wasn't a big deal, that TV networks hand out titles like they do gold watches. Moore didn't believe him. His friend happened to work for the National Biscuit Company and said, "We have over at our company a vice-president in charge of fig newtons." Moore didn't believe it. His friend said, "Call over there and ask for him."

So Moore took the phone and called the National Biscuit Company and said, "I'd like to speak to the Vice-President in charge of fig newtons." He was shocked when the receptionist said, "Is that packaged fig newtons or bulk fig newtons?"[3]

Too many of us struggle and strive to receive the earthly titles. We strive to be something in the eyes of the world, but in the long run it will disappoint us. We will never be at peace with ourselves. Christmas comes to tell us that we are the children of God, and we'd better start with that. He made us. He loves us. We have value. We have worth because we are his.

What we are expected to do is not to live up to what another person is but to the ability that we have. We're not in competition with one another. We're to be in cooperation with one another. We're not to be what another is. We're not to live up to their gifts. All we are asked to do is to live up to what we can be under God, to live up to our potential with his help. Others ought not to threaten us. Others ought not to frighten us. We are to be the child of God that we can be. There's no one like us, no one with our gifts and talents. All we have to be is ourselves.

I read the story of a little boy who was born with sicknesses and deformities. He couldn't talk, he couldn't walk, he couldn't use his hands. He had to live in a wheelchair. But it's the story of how teachers worked with him over a period of years to try to get him to develop some of his muscles to be able to push himself up out of the wheelchair.

To help him develop the use of his hands, they gave him a loom to try to weave some pot holders. His hands were very out of control, and often the loops would be thrown all over the room. But he stayed with it and the pot holder began to take shape. He would come in every morning and hold that partly made pot holder close to him because it was his creation.

On his eleventh birthday, he'd learned to put his tools away. He had progressed from what he was and what they expected him to be. He indicated to one of the workers that he wanted to write something.

She gave him a piece of paper and very painstakingly he scribbled some words, turned and showed them to her. They were very hard to see. You know what that little boy wrote? Four words! "I'm proud of myself."[4]

Here was a boy who couldn't walk, couldn't talk, who couldn't do what others did, but he was proud of himself because he was not judging himself by what others did; he was judging himself by what he was able to do and how he was able to grow. He had accepted himself as he was, and he knew what it was to be at peace. It is boys like that who will win the world and not the Herods with all of their insecurity, no matter what they have.

Christmas comes to tell us that if we ever want life to be what it ought to be, we've got to start by accepting ourselves as the children of God. All we're expected to do is live up to what God wants us to be. Are we living up to our potential? That's what Christmas wants to know.

2. Christmas can become a curse when we never deal with our sin.

Herod was a cruel person. He killed members of his family in order to make sure that he kept his throne. But what a terrible deed he did here! Babies, innocent, tiny baby boys, two years and under—he had them massacred and he didn't seem to care. How could he do that? He could do it because the power of sin and evil had overtaken him. He had not learned to fight against it or deal with it. Instead, he gave into it and it had hold of him. He couldn't break its power, or didn't want to.

Christmas is a reminder that there is something in our lives that keeps us from being what we want to be. We remember Christmas. We remember those feelings we had when we were younger. They were great feelings of love and how we were going to grow up and give love to all people. We were going to be the lovers that this world needed in order to make it a better place.

Christmas reminds us that we haven't always done that. Christmas was a time when we sang of "peace on earth, goodwill to men" and that was what we were going to do. We were going to go about trying to bring peace to this world. We were going to go about trying to make the world a better place by being good and helping people.

Christmas reminds us of those commitments we made to God a long time ago. We were going to serve him and love him and follow him, but between then and now we see that we have not always kept our dreams. Why not? The problem is that the power of sin has attacked us and we have given in. We have failed. We have fallen. It's very disturbing to know that. It's very disturbing to be told we have not become what we intended or wanted. Christmas asks us, "Why not? What's the problem?"

The problem is that we have underestimated the power of sin. We underestimate what it can do to us, how strong a hold it can get on us, how difficult it will be to break sin's hold on us. We know that we have fallen far short of what we meant to be. What can we do about it? Christmas tells us that there is a way out of our sin. There is a way to deal positively with our sin, and here it is.

We must give our sins to the Christ who came for them. This is why Christ came. He came to take upon himself the sins of the world, to offer all of us forgiveness and the chance to be free again. That's it. We can't go back and change the past. Christ is more concerned about tomorrow. What will we do about it?

Cecil Myers, a pastor in Georgia, was asked by a doctor to visit a seventy-three-year-old woman. She was in the hospital but the doctor could find no organic problems with her. He sensed that there was something more to it. As Myers visited with her, he discovered that there was a great guilt that this woman had been carrying with her for over fifty years.

She had been in love with a young man. They were engaged to be married. They had committed some premarital indiscretions. He had broken the engagement eventually and left her. All through her life, even though she had married another man and had had several children, she kept this a secret. She kept the guilt of it alive and it grew and grew.

Myers said, "Christ has taught that if we confess our sins, he is just to forgive us and cleanse us from all unrighteousness. Do you believe that? Do you believe with all faith that if you confess your sins Christ will forgive them? Do you believe that?" That's what he asked this woman. As he prayed with her, he put his hand on her and said, "Your sins are forgiven," and for the first time in her life, she believed they were. That afternoon she left the hospital, cured of the guilt that had been keeping her from being what she ought to be.[5]

The same thing can happen to you. Do you believe that Christ will forgive your sins? Because if you do I have the joy to tell you that if you turn them over to him, they will be forgiven. You don't have to go around punishing yourself anymore for the mistakes you've made. All you need to do is head for tomorrow with a new chance and a new start.

3. Christmas can become a curse when we won't believe love is the way to life.

Herod didn't believe in such a sissy thing as love. To him the cure for all the problems was force and violence. So you take a sword and chop off the head of some baby boy and all of the problems that he faced would be taken away. Force, power, violence—that was Herod's way.

There was born at that time a Christ who would say that it was not the way. The way to life was not through force or violence, it was through love, self-giving, sacrificial love. Herod didn't believe it. The world didn't.

Some thirty years later, there was a great confrontation: Pilate with all the power of the Roman army and his position on one side and Christ with only the offer of love. Which one would you have bet on that day? Pilate or Christ?

It is Christ's way. Suffering, sacrificial love carried the day. Jesus told us himself, "I have overcome the world." Do we believe that? Not really. What do we think we need to solve all of our problems? Is it power? If we just had more bullets and bombs, we could solve the problems of the world. Is it more knowledge? If we had more human ingenuity and technological advances we could solve all of our problems. What do we think can solve the problems of the world?

Surely not love that is unconditional. Surely not love that seeks the best for others. Surely not love that says to love your enemies. Not that! You know what will happen if we went through this world trying to love people? We might get crucified! Just like Christ!

Do you know what Christ tried to tell us? You can take the love of God and nail it to a cross, but it's going to keep coming after you. You can't kill it. It keeps after you. It keeps coming. "Love," he said, "is the way."

There was a young man from Georgia who got his orders from the army. He'd never been far away from his farm in Georgia. It was a new life to him. He was very devout. Every night he would read his Bible and get on his knees and say his prayers before he went to bed. That irritated his sergeant who didn't agree with that way of life and sought to make the boy over in his own image. Through basic training, he would verbally abuse the young man and have him do unjust punishments because he wouldn't respond favorably to what he wanted him to be. But no matter what he made him do, the soldier never retaliated in anger. In fact, he would take every occasion he could find to try to do something good for the sergeant.

One night the sergeant came in drunk, and the boy was saying his prayers at his bed. This made the sergeant raging mad. He began to verbally abuse him, yell and scream at him, but the boy just stayed there on his knees saying his prayers. Finally, the sergeant was so mad that he took off one of his muddy boots and hurled it at the young man, hitting him on the back of the head and knocking him down into the floor. He just got back up and went on praying. The sergeant got his other boot off and did the same thing. The soldier continued to pray.

Finally, the sergeant stumbled off to bed. When he woke up in the morning fighting off his hangover, the first thing he saw was two freshly shined boots under his bunk. He couldn't take it any more and ran up to this boy and said, "What is it with you? I have tried everything I know to break you, to make you be like me. But you've never been able to fall. What is it you know? What's the secret of your humanity? I want to know!"[6]

It's no secret. It's been out for thousands of years. The secret is the love of Christ that dwells within. I don't think his love has been tried and found wanting. We just haven't tried it enough. We haven't loved like Christ enough. Until we learn to love that way, we will never know the joy and deep happiness of life that is ours for the taking. Christmas will never be Christmas until we dedicate ourselves to the way of Christ's sacrificial love.

Give Herod credit for one thing. He knew that he had to take Christ seriously. He either had to follow him or destroy him. He tried the latter way. There are many today who find Christmas to be a curse simply because they have not faced up to Christ. They have not trusted him.

Whenever we do not give ourselves in complete trust to Christ, the songs, the deeds and the worship of Christmas will make us uneasy inside. But there's the other side. If we trust him with every ounce of faith that we have in us, accept ourselves as his children, accept the gifts of forgiveness he has for us and strive to live the way of love, then we can begin to know a little about what he brought at Christmas. Christmas will not be a curse. It will be a cure: a cure for our fears, our insecurities, our hate, our misery. That's what Christmas is supposed to mean. Christmas is about a Christ who can cure all of our ills and give us life abundant, life eternal, life now.

If you want it you have to start where every one of us starts, by worshiping this Christ who came at Bethlehem, worshiping him as Savior and Lord! If we live for him, one day we will shout at

Christmastime or in the middle of July, "Hosanna, Blessed is he who comes! He is King of kings, Lord of lords of our lives."

NOTES

1. *Pulpit Resources* (Oct.-Dec. 1977), p. 29.

2. Thomas Hilton, "Keeping the Mass in Christmas," *The Clergy Journal* (Nov.-Dec. 1971), p. 10.

3. *Pulpit Resource* (first quarter, 1976), p. 11.

4. Paul E. Vandine, "God of Many Majesties: But Mostly Love," *Master Sermons*, May 1978, p. 247.

5. T. Cecil Myers, *Living on Tiptoe* (Waco: Word, 1972), p. 29.

6. John Claypool, "The Beast and The Lamb," Sermon: Broadway Baptist Church, Fort Worth, Texas, 8 Feb. 1976, pp. 1-2.

THE WISE MEN

Being Caught by a Vision

(Matt. 2:1-12)

Some years ago underneath the Brooklyn Bridge on the Manhattan side, there stood an old, deserted tobacco warehouse. It had become a shelter to hundreds of the derelicts of the city—those down on their luck.

The city of New York asked the Salvation Army to do something for them. They provided some bowls of soup and some coffee. One day, Joseph Sizoo, a preacher, was asked to speak to them, a very difficult thing to do. Those broken pieces of humanity just stared at him with empty eyes.

After the service, one man came up to him and said, "Do you read Greek?" Sizoo said, "Yes, I do." "Do you know how to read the Greek New Testament?" "Yes, I do." Sizoo said, "Let's read it together." The man protested, but after a while this story came out.

This fellow with the long hair, a stubby beard, and a very shabby coat held together by string and a nail had at one time been a teacher of New Testament Greek in a college. He was an excellent teacher, well respected. He became dean of the faculty. He had a lovely wife and three children and was a very active person, involved in the community and in his church.

But something happened to him. He began to lose sight of the right values. He began to lose perspective about what life was all about. Before long, things came down hard on him; he turned to the bottle and before he knew it he was an alcoholic. Here he was in New York City in a tobacco warehouse, with no family, no friends, no money, no work; and it seemed to him, no hope.[1]

Unfortunately, there are this Christmas too many sad stories just like that. There are people who have made a mess of their lives, people who have found life to be too hard for them and who have given up, people who have had their dreams and hopes dashed to pieces. How can we keep that from happening to us? How can we keep from becoming those who are among the world's "hopeless?" How can we keep from coming to the end of our lives only to look back to see that we never really lived?

It can happen to us, you know. There may be some of you who are struggling desperately to find something worthwhile and meaningful in life. There may be those of you who are depressed about the way life has been treating you. Some of you may be tempted to give up, forget it, and leave it all behind. You may be wandering aimlessly, searching for life but not knowing where to find it. How in the world can life become alive for you? What's the secret? Where is the key? Does Christmas have a word for you?

So enter into our Christmas story the Wise Men. To be truthful, we don't know much about them. We don't really know how many there were. The Bible doesn't tell us. It may have been more than three; we think there were three because of the number of gifts.

We don't know who they were. Most scholars feel they were Persian priests who had made a hobby of studying magic and astrology. We don't even know when they got there to see Christ. Matthew tells us they found him in a house maybe that night or anywhere up to two years.

But what we do know about the Wise Men is this: they had a vision that a Messiah would be born into the world. They were willing to follow that vision, and nothing would stop them from it. Here was the key to their lives. They were caught by a vision worth giving their lives to.

Here is the key for every one of our lives. If you and I want to really live and keep from becoming those broken pieces of humanity that so often lie around us, we need to be caught by a vision. Christmas comes down to tell us what the vision is all about.

1. We need to be caught by a vision that's worthy to live for.

The Wise Men saw the star and followed it. They followed it because they believed it would lead them to the King of the Jews, the new Messiah, the one who would bring peace and brotherhood to the world. They believed that vision. They were willing to follow it, whatever the price, however far they had to go. They believed it was worth giving their lives for. It was their purpose to find this King.

We've got to have such a purpose, too. An old story tells of an African woman who went out into the jungle. She was about to give birth to a child. There in the mist a figure appeared to her and said, "If I touch you, your child will have wealth." She said, "No." Another shape appeared and said, "If I touch you, your child will have fame," and she said, "No." Another form said, "If I touch you, your child will have happiness," and she shook her head no.

Many other shapes appeared to her but finally a shape appeared and said, "If I touch you, your child will hear a voice calling him from beyond the hills and he will feel led to go out to it and to chase it. All during his life, he will never touch it, but there will burn deep inside of him that light that he must chase and he will brave anything to chase it." The woman said, "Touch me."[2]

Do you have any such purpose or light burning in your life? What is it that we shape our lives around? For we were all meant to have some purpose, some vision, some God that we will seek. The world offers us many purposes, many ways to give our lives, many visions to follow.

We can seek money. We can seek prestige. We can seek power. We can seek pleasure. Come, they beckon to us. They promise us life, but will they deliver? The purposes we are living for now if we achieve them, will they fulfill us? Will we be satisfied if we get now what we're after?

Christmas tries to tell us that there is a purpose that's worth living for: a worthy purpose called the kingdom of God. That's the star that you and I need to seek and to strive for: a Kingdom where all people are under the lordship and love of God, where everybody works together to try to bring love and joy and brotherhood and peace.

Christmas comes to tell us that we can join in that vision by following the Christ who brings it. Each one of us, if we wish, can dedicate ourselves to the purpose of finding the kingdom of God here on earth as it is in heaven. It is a purpose that will burn in our souls and will never be satisfied as long as we live.

It talks about ending prejudice and bigotry and hatred among all people; about bringing peace in the world; about stopping poverty, hunger, and illiteracy; about fighting disease and sickness; about standing tall and fighting against injustice and wrong. You can do that and you will never dedicate your life to worthier goals. But it's a lifetime task. Work as hard as you may, do as much as you can and the light will still beckon you. There is more to do. But what else is worthier than that? To try to bring God's kingdom here on earth is the highest purpose to live for.

Loren Eisley, who served as provost of the University of Pennsylvania, wrote in his autobiography about a time when he was interviewed by a reporter who asked him what was his most significant act as provost at Pennsylvania. He said, "I made my contribution to the spectral war."

The reporter didn't know what he was talking about so Eisley took him down to Walnut and 34th Streets, right across from Bennett Hall. He said, "See that street there?" There was a street that went way out to make a left turn with a stop sign.

He said, "When I came here, there was no long, square corner there. There was only a quick curve. Cabbies and truckers and all the people who came down that street would come down and quickly cut across that curve, right in the middle of the university. It was dangerous for our students. I personally witnessed five injuries and saw one woman being run down by a truck.

"So I found out when the meeting was—when they talked about traffic conditions on campus and at that meeting I used all my influence and all my power to get it changed. The taxicab drivers didn't like it. The truck drivers didn't like it. Nobody seemed to like it, but I was able to change it so now that street goes out a little further and there is a stop sign so they would have to stop. It took longer for them to go through that place."

The reporter said, "Is that all you remember about being provost?" "That I don't know, but I'd like to believe that because that street is longer now, that there are people alive today who would not have been alive otherwise."[3]

That is the spectral war. It is an unseen war. It is the constant struggle in trying to make this world a better place. But I say to you, that if you want something worth living for, do that.

2. We need to be caught by a vision that will not die, no matter what.

The trip was a long one for the Wise Men. It wasn't an overnight trip. I am sure they got tired and weary and wanted to quit, but they believed in the vision too much for that. They stopped in Jerusalem to find out what the Jews thought about this new one to be born.

Herod found out about it and wanted to know when the baby was going to be born and where. They knew that Herod was not honest, that he was scared of the baby. So they didn't go back to him and that was dangerous. To defy the king could mean your life. But they didn't go back because they believed in the vision too much. Whatever the risk, they would do everything they could to see that it would not be destroyed, that it would last forever.

This is something that we will discover on the way to our vision. Following our star will not always be easy. The road to the end of our rainbows are often filled with loneliness and disappointment and discouragement, obstacles of all kind. Far too many people have started out after a vision; but, when the difficulties came in trying to reach it, they would quit or compromise for less than their vision.

We know that this is true, for all we have to do is think back to our younger days when we started out with our ideals and visions. All the things we were going to be and do. How kind and good and how caring we were going to be. When we came down to the altar and committed our life to Christ, we were going to be the best Christians that we could ever be. We were going to be good marriage partners, good parents. We were going to be involved in the church, doing all we could to see it live. How many promises did we make? How many stars did we set out to follow? But like that man who taught Greek, visions can sometimes be lost.

Why? There are lots of reasons. Maybe it's because of the criticism we get when we try to do what we think is right. Maybe it's because of the hurt that comes when we try to love and our love is rejected. Maybe it's because of discouragement that comes when we try to do what we think is right for God and it doesn't seem to do any good. Maybe it's just the frustration of trying to live in this world with all of its bills, taxes, sickness, and pain.

Often the tragedy of so many people's lives is that they have quit following their vision, given up on their star. Have you? Those who do settle for less than the best usually settle in to routine and boredom and misery. Those who give up on their stars lose out on life. It must not be! We believed in our vision once. We believed that it was the best vision possible. Don't we still? We must never give up on it! We must never let it die!

Winston Churchill, speaking at his old school, thought about that time when he was a child and used to stammer and would not even think of speaking in front of people. But now he was one of the great orators of the time. He had overcome that difficulty because he had a vision that he could. His word of advice to those students was, "Never give up, never, never, never!"[4]

3. If we keep our vision going, we will reach it.

The wise men followed the star because they thought it would lead them to the Messiah and it did. Their vision did not disappoint them to the Messiah and it did. Their vision did not disappoint them. The star was right and they fell down and worshiped the Christ. They had found who they were looking for. They went home another way, not only literally but also another way inside because they had found their Lord. No longer would life be the same for them. The vision was true!

This is what Christmas tries to tell us. The vision of the kingdom of God is true. Peace on earth, "good will toward men," the angels sang (Luke 2:14, KJV). One day you will find that it's true. Emmanuel, God with us. That is true, now and forever! The brotherhood of Christmas, shepherds and Wise Men, the down and out and the up and in gather to worship the Christ. One day it will be like that. The hope of Christmas that the suffering and the darkness and death will one day be gone is true! Christmas tells us that the vision of the kingdom of God that Christ brought will come to be. All other visions will not. Any vision without God will fail, whether it's based upon our love of ourselves or of money or of pleasure or power. All other visions will fail.

The only wisdom that will last will be the kingdom of God. We can believe that and live for it. We can know that every step we take is not in vain if it's toward God. We can know that every word we speak in his behalf is not lost. We can know that every deed we do for his sake is not forgotten. All we do will help bring the kingdom of God closer to reality. It is a vision worth living for. One day we will discover the kingdom of God in all of its fullness. We must ever be thankful to the vision because if we are faithful to that vision, God will let us have it.

I read of a girl who was writing of her Christmas. When she was eight years old her father had died and there wasn't much money in the home and the mother had to work. Christmas came and they just didn't have many presents. The other kids had bikes and wagons and big toys. She and her sister just had a little rubber doll; the boy had a toy car. Both gifts cost less than a dollar apiece. She remembered the depression, and the feeling of sadness and emptiness she felt. It seemed that she was left out. Someone had forgotten her.

But in between her eighth and ninth year, a Mrs. Brown came into their lives and loved them and cared for them and ministered to them. That next Christmas, there was a station wagon full of toys and bikes, and they knew what Christmas was about in the sense of receiving love and joy. "That Christmas," she said, "I remember going in to my mother and saying with tears rolling down my cheeks, 'Mother, Christmas is for real.'"[5]

And it is. All the joy, all the love, and all the peace and goodwill we sing about, it's real! It's for real, and if we follow that star, one day we will know it.

The trouble with the man at the New York warehouse was that he had lost his dreams. But there was still hope for him. Christmas reminds us that the star is still shining. Christ can still be found and dreams can be recaptured and followed again.

What some of us need is to sift through the ashes of forgotten dreams, to let be born again in our lives a new determination and a commitment to follow the vision of the kingdom of God. We do that by doing what these Wise Men of old did and the wise men of every age do, and that is to fall down and worship this newborn King we know as Jesus Christ and to follow him with every ounce of faith in us. It will keep us from coming to the point when we look back on our lives and say, "We never lived."

See the Christmas star? It points to Christ. Keep him in your vision, and onward go!

NOTES

1. Joseph R. Sizoo, *Still We Can Hope* (Nashville: Abingdon Press, 1966), pp. 97-99.

2. J. Wallace Hamilton, "What Makes the Church?" Sermon: Pasadena Community Church, Saint Petersburg, Florida, 13 Mar. 1960, p. 13.

3. Daryl Fleming, "The Spectral War," *Master Sermons*, Aug. 1979, pp. 406-407.

4. Norman Vincent Peale, *White House Sermons*, ed. by Ben Hibbs (New York: Harper and Row, 1972), p. 60.

5. Earl R. Eckhart, "I Don't Believe It," *Master Sermons*, Dec. 1980, p. 571.

MARY AND JOSEPH

Carrying Christmas into Life

(Matt. 2:19-23)

In one of the Peanuts cartoons, Lucy comes to Charlie Brown and says, "Merry Christmas. Since it's this time of the season, I think we ought to bury past differences and try to be kind." Charlie Brown said, "Why does it just have to be this time of the season? Why can't it be all year long?" Lucy looked at him and said, "What are you, some kind of fanatic?"[1]

I hear us saying, "Wouldn't it be wonderful if Christmas could last all year long," for we don't expect it to. It's a pipe dream. We know it. Already most of us have come down off those mountaintops of joy and good times, and we're back into the valley of trying to struggle for a living.

Christmas doesn't last. Someone likened it to jumping out of a plane with a parachute. For a moment, when the parachute opens and you soar suspended in the sky, it's a magnificent feeling. But it doesn't last. Before too long, your feet come pounding to the ground and it's back to business as usual.[2]

Business as usual. Will this be the way it is for us in the days ahead? Can it be that? Can it ever be business as usual after we have once again gone through the Christmas experience? Do you think it was business as usual for the shepherds and Wise Men after they saw the child? Do you think it was business as usual for Mary and Joseph after the experience of Christmas?

After we have sung the songs and worshiped at Christmas, after we have thought again of the meaning of Christmas, can we go back with indifference to our work not changed at all? Or has Christmas possibly burned a new fire and a new hope into our bones and we know somehow that life can't be the same? Is there any possibility for you and me to carry Christmas into life?

47

Mary and Joseph had to do it. The shepherds and the Wise Men and the angels and the star—all of that was wonderful, but there came that moment when they were all gone, and Mary and Joseph were left alone with their new child, left alone with a tremendous responsibility of having to take this child and help him to become what God wanted him to be. In a sense, they had the responsibility to take what they learned at Christmas and bring it into life. So do we. But how do we go about doing it? What does it mean to carry Christmas into life?

1. We must carry Christmas into the home.

Mary and Joseph had to do that. Parents of the Christ child! What a tremendous privilege and what an awesome responsibility! They had to help Jesus to grow up to understand the importance of God and of doing his will. That was not easy.

I am sure that Jesus was like any other baby and any other boy. I am sure he got sick in the night and cried and kept them up. I am sure there were times when he got into a little mischief. I'm sure he wiggled and squirmed in the synagogue services, like most children do. I'm sure there were probably those times when he didn't pick up his clothes or clean his teeth before he went to bed. Maybe there were those times when he didn't listen to them when they tried to tell him about God and about all that he meant in their lives.

But they tried. They tried to teach him. They took him to church. They read him the Scriptures. They told him what they knew. But more importantly, they lived their faith in the home. Through it all, Jesus heard. We read later in Scripture that he grew "in wisdom and in stature, and in favor with God and man" (Luke 2:52). Somewhere along the line, Christ understood what he was supposed to be and do. Christmas caught hold of Christ for one reason because Mary and Joseph took that significant meaning of Christmas and lived it in the home.

We often talk about Christmastimes of the past. Most of the time we talk about our families. We remember the good times when we were with the ones we loved and how nice it felt. This Christmas, many of your families got together again. You had reunions. How good it was, that feeling of togetherness and how you wished you could keep it. But it won't be easy. In order for us to keep the spirit of love and joy and peace and hope that we feel at Christmas alive, we've got to keep it in the home. We've got to teach it to one another. We've got to live it in the home. It is no secret. If our children are to grow up to understand all that Christmas means, they're going to learn it first of all in the home.

The world's greatest theological school is the home. More is learned about God in the home than any other place. By what we teach our children, by our attitudes and the way we live at home, they will learn about God and how important or how unimportant he is. One of the tremendous responsibilities we have is to carry the Christmas spirit into our homes and live it.

What have we carried into our homes? We talk about the love of Christmas. Are we loving one another in the home? Are we treating each other there as persons or as things? We talk about hope. Are we hopeful persons, or are we very pessimistic about the way things are and about the way people are? We talk about the significance of God. How significant is he in our lives? Is worship something we do when we have nothing else to do? Do we involve ourselves in his ministry and in his service?

What concerns me as pastor is that many in our children's departments and many young people have parents who are not involved in the church at all. I think the sin of that will come home to roost one day. More often than not, they will grow up with a disinterest in the matters of faith. What are we teaching in the home? What are we living in the home? All that we celebrate at Christmas, all that we feel at Christmas— are we going to try to live it all year long?

Chevis Horne, who was president of our Virginia Baptist Convention, told of a time he visited the Amish in Pennsylvania. The Amish have rebelled against modern technology and refuse to be overcome by it. They still ride around in horse-drawn carriages. They don't have anything to do with modern conveniences. We would consider them old-fashioned and out-of-date.

He visited in one of the homes and was talking about seeing a kindly grandmother with two grandchildren, one eight, one four. He asked her, "What is the greatest hope you have for your grandchildren?" Quick as a flash she said, "That they may know, love and serve Jesus Christ."[3]

What is the greatest hope we have for our children in our homes? That they may be successful in the eyes of the world? Beautiful or popular, rich? What is our greatest hope for our children? Is it that they know, love, and serve Jesus Christ? If Christmas has meant anything to us, our greatest desire should be that those we love most will know, love, and serve Jesus Christ. Christmas will never live in the world until we live it in our homes.

2. We must carry Christmas into our workaday worlds.

Mary and Joseph had to survive, and it wasn't easy for them. We know Joseph was a carpenter. That was hard work, and it didn't pay too much. They were poor, the parents of Christ. But somehow, they survived through the hard work they were able to do. Somehow, I feel that after Christmas, the work they did took on a new significance and a new importance. Now they knew that they were servants of God. He needed them. He was using them. They were important to him. They would provide Jesus an atmosphere in which he could grow up with a sense of security and love.

I feel that Joseph's hammer was not as heavy and his saw sawed a little bit easier. The clothes to wash and the meals to cook were not as hard for Mary to do. They both understood that they were offering service to God through their work. What they did was being used by God, every nail that he hammered, every pot that she cleaned. Jesus learned to be a carpenter, got blisters on his hands, brought honor and glory to human work, knowing that it could be used not only to serve others but to serve God.

Most of us are looking toward going back to work after Christmas, but not with a sense of excitement and joy. It is routine and boring for many. But back to work we must go, back to the ships and the typewriters and the classrooms and the hammers and the saws. Soon the Christmas music and the Christmas hope will be lost as we struggle and sweat to survive. But does it have to be that way after we have listened again to the fact that God has come to dwell in the midst of this world? As we remember that this is his world and it is sacred, maybe, just maybe, we can begin to understand that what we do is important to God also.

All we do can be offered up to God as an offering. Maybe what we do he will take and use it to better others and to make the world a better place to live in. Maybe work doesn't have to be so boring if we understand that it is an offering to God. What will God do with it? I don't know. But would it make a difference in your life and work if the letters you typed, the truth you taught, the goods you sold, the hammers and the saws you used were offered to God? Unfortunately we often do work to make a living and that is not the primary purpose of work.

Work ought to be an offering to God, an offering that will help to contribute to the betterment of this world, to the betterment of others. God will be there to help you do that. He will use that.

St. Anthony was a very devout man, but somebody told him there was a man more devout than he was. He wanted to find out who this man was so he could learn the secret of his life. He was a cobbler in another town. He said, "Tell me, what is the secret of your devout life?" The man said, "I have no secret, but I'll tell you what I do. I make shoes, and every shoe I make, I make for Jesus Christ."[4]

I wonder if that would make any difference in your lives? If by you on the assembly line, sitting next to you in your classrooms, standing next to you and your typewriter, next to you on the ship, you imagine God there taking what you offer and using it? You see, Christmas is for all of life. It is for your work because it reminds you that God can use it because it is his world and his life, and he needs it. Work ought never to be the same again because in Bethlehem, Christ was born.

3. We must carry Christmas into the area of our faith.

Mary and Joseph would need to remember Bethlehem often because there would be those moments in their lives when their faith in God would be sorely tested and tried. They would have to run for their lives to the strange land of Egypt. There were hard and difficult times in their lives when I'm sure they wondered where God was.

We know that Joseph died and Mary was left alone with the tremendous responsibility of bringing up their children. Had God deserted her then? There were surely those moments when she could have thought so, but one of our Scriptures reports the fact that Mary pondered all these things "in her heart."

Mary remembered the Christmas event. She needed to because when everything seemed to point to the fact that God had forgotten her, she would know that it was not so. She could remember there at Bethlehem God had not forgotten anyone, that he was at work in the world in ways that no one could really see. She didn't know how, but she lived by that faith and trusted that God was there.

There is no doubt that many of us will go away from this Christmas season and land in some "Egypt" where our faith will be tested. Maybe it will be the death of a loved one that will break our hearts. Maybe it will be sickness that will not go away. Maybe it will be a frustrating disappointment, a job we didn't get, a love that's rejected. Maybe we'll just find ourselves bored with the way life is. But life will come down hard on us and in the middle of it we will begin to wonder, where's God anyway? All those songs we sang at Christmas about God being in the midst of the world, where is he?

That's when we'll need to remember Christmas. We'll need to remember that Christmas tells us that where he is is where we are. We may not always see his presence, we may not always know how he is working his will in our lives, but Christmas tells us that he is. We are not forgotten. We're not alone. In the midst of our difficult, trying moments, we need to remember Bethlehem—that God has come. We must never give up on that; we must never lose hold of that. We must hold on to it with every ounce of faith we have in us. For that is what will keep us going on and on.

There's a painting in New York of a group of travelers climbing a mountain. The mountain is steep and hard to climb. There are stones on the road, thorns all along it, and the band of travelers are tired; some are bruised and some are bleeding. Their way up the mountain is slowed down by the fact that they have to help each other up.

But what are they heading for? On the other side of the mountain, beyond their sight, the artist has painted all the beauty he could in the City of God. They're heading for that, but they cannot see it. How can they keep going up that mountain with all of the terrible struggles that they had?

Then they see that high in the clouds above that City of God was etched the face of Jesus Christ. They could keep on going in the midst of the thorns and the stones and the tiredness and the difficulty because their eyes were fixed on Jesus Christ.[5]

Christmas tells us that we can go on and on in the face of all our difficulties as long as we keep our eyes on the face of this Christ who has come to dwell with us. He knows the way. He is the way. Keep your eyes on him and never lose heart.

So the Christmas season is over. The decorations will be gone before too long. The trees will come down. But while the Christmas season is over and Christmas day is over, Christmas must never end. It must live, for Christmas is all about Christ helping us live at home and at work. We must never lose sight of him. If we don't, in the days ahead we will walk with a new step, a new hope and a new joy because we will have once again been reminded that Jesus Christ is alive and in the world.

Howard Thurman, the great black preacher, wrote these words: "When the song of the angels is stilled, when the star in the sky is gone, when the kings and princes are home, when the shepherds are back with their flocks, the work of Christmas begins. To find the lost, to heal the broken, to feed the hungry, to release the prisoner, to rebuild the nations, to bring peace among sisters and brothers, to make music in the heart."[6]

The reason we can do every one of those tasks is because Christ has come to help us every day. Christmas can be every day.

NOTES

1. Robert C. Shannon, "Season's Greetings," *Pulpit Digest* (Nov.-Dec. 1979), p. 11.

2. William Sloane Coffin, Jr., "They Returned Home Another Way," Sermon: Riverside Church, New York, New York, 8 Jan. 1978, p. 1.

3. Chevis Horne, *Being Christian in Our Town* (Nashville: Broadman Press, 1978), pp. 104-105.

4. Brian Harbour, "Workers Whom God Approves," *Pulpit Digest* (Sept.-Oct. 1980), p. 40.

5. Clarence W. Cranford, "The Pull of the Beyond," *Toward Authentic Morality for Modern Man*, Proceedings of the Christian Life Commission Seminar, Southern Baptist Convention, Atlanta, Georgia, 1970, p. 17.

6. Howard Thurman, *Pulpit Resource*, (Oct.-Dec. 1979), p. 37.

Series Two
Christmas Music

Music is a major portion of the Christmas story. A look at the Scriptures reveals four basic hymns or songs that are contained in the recounting of the events surrounding that first Christmas. It provides a good theme for a series on Christmas. I have also included a Christmas Eve communion service in this series to illustrate how it can be tied in to the general theme.

Sermons

Mary's Song: The God of the Lowly
Zechariah's Song: What God Means
The Angel's Song: The Dream We Covet
Christ's Song: A Love for All Seasons
Simeon's Song: Catching Christmas

The God of the Lowly

(Luke 1:46-55)

The statement was made on a television show that it was the Christmas season again and the collective response of the audience was one loud groan. There was something about the Christmas season that caused them to feel pain. What was it?

Maybe they were remembering all the Christmas presents they had to buy and wrap, the crowds they had to fight, the cards they had to address, the decorations to do, the parties to go to. Maybe remembering all the busy activities of the Christmas season made them feel like groaning.

Christmas is a busy time. We get caught up in it too; and at times, I hear our groans being lifted to heaven. But if it's so frightening, so frustrating, so bothersome, why do we bother? Why do we take the time to be involved in all of the many activities that Christmas brings about? I hope it's because we know what Christmas is *all* about, that we know what it means.

Christmas means that this is a God-invaded world: Christ has come to be with us now and forever. Since it is a God-invaded world, it changes the way we look at life and the world and everything. When we remember that Christmas means that God is with us, instead of a groan it ought to cause us to utter a shout of gratitude.

We can miss it. We can get so involved in all of the activities and the commercialism that we find ourselves pushing Christ to the fringes of our Christmas celebration. That must not happen. That is why we try to help you to celebrate Christmas through many activities of worship, recreation, and music. We want to remember that Christmas without Christ is not Christmas at all.

Our theme for our Christmas celebration this year is "Christmas Music." The first song we want to hear is the song of Mary, that simple, devout, peasant girl who grew up in Nazareth. Many scholars feel that she was twelve years old when she discovered that she was going to be the mother of the Christ child. It was an overwhelming experience for her as you might imagine.

From her joy, she sang the song we call the Magnificat. She rejoiced in the God that she had discovered in her experience. The interesting thing is that the God she discovered was a God who was for the lowly. Throughout the song, she described a God who was concerned about those no one else seemed to be concerned for.

If we're ever going to celebrate Christmas right, we've got to understand the kind of God who came. We need to look at her song and see how God is a God for the lowly.

1. He is a God who came to love the forgotten.

This was what stunned Mary, that God would want *her* for his holy task. "He has regarded the low estate of his handmaiden" (v. 48). Mary wasn't worthy. Mary didn't deserve it. But somehow God wanted her. She talked about the fact that He has "exalted those of low degree" (v. 52). The forgotten, the helpless, the powerless, the needy—those were the ones that God cared about. They were the ones he was going to bring the good news to.

"He has helped," she said, "his servant Israel" (v. 54), that ragtag group of Jewish people who had rebelled so many times and were scattered abroad and seemed so helpless. He cared for them, too. All through her song is the indication of a God who knew those everyone else had forgotten about, who cared for those everyone else had passed by on the other side. He was the God who loved the unlovely. That's why he came.

It is interesting at Christmas that we do seem to have concerted efforts made to meet the needs of the poor and the less fortunate. With our Christmas baskets and our Toys for Tots and our Joy Fund, we try to meet the needs of those whose Christmas might not be quite as good as ours.

Why do we do it at Christmas time? I think because there's a feeling inside that the God who came at Christmas is a God who loves these people, and because he loved them so should we. So at Christmas, there seems to be a heightening of our sensitivities to each other's needs.

It's so sad that the rest of the year these same needs are often ignored or forgotten. This is why Christ did come. He came to go to those who felt themselves unworthy, to go to those who felt themselves forgotten and left out, and to tell them they were not left out. They were cared about, and they were understood. He came to identify with them.

A mother and her daughter, dressed in shabby clothes, were standing outside one of the big department stores, admiring the manger scene in the window. It was a big manger scene with the Wise Men and their lavish gifts, Mary and Joseph, and the Christ child. The little girl kept staring at the face of Mary, that white plaster face, so pure. Finally, the little girl said, "She's so beautiful, but she doesn't know the pain and trouble that we have."[1]

What Christ came down at Christmas to say to that little girl and all those like her in the world is that God knows all the pain and trouble that she faces. For Christ came down to go to these people, to share·with them, to bear their burdens, to suffer the same sufferings they did. Christ is not separated from the pain and the loneliness and the heartbreak that so many people feel at Christmas. He has been there, he knows. He understands, and he cares.

The Word becomes flesh in our lives, too. God makes his trip into our common ways as well. I remember a simple woodcut that caught this truth. At the top of the woodcut was the star of Bethlehem, its light shining into the city below. But the city was not Bethlehem; it was a modern city with tall buildings and factories. In the foreground a road led to the city, and people were traveling toward the star: not the shepherds, not the wise men, but a soldier, a priest, a factory worker, a housewife—men and women in modern dress.[2]

In a sense, this is what God has come to say at Christmas. The same concern he has for the rich, he has for the poor. The same concern he has for the "up and ins" he has for the "down and outs." The same concern he has for the powerful, he has for the weak. Everyone is precious to him. That means, thank God, you and me.

2. God is a God who comes to have mercy on the needy.

This was another part of Mary's song. He has mercy on "those who fear Him" (v. 50). Those who trusted him, those who believed in him, those who committed themselves to him—God was merciful to them. They needed it.

These Jewish people had rebelled so many times, broken the heart of God over and over, but there were still those who clung somehow to the belief that God would not forget them; God would still come and make out of them something worthwhile. Mary knew that God would. From her experience, she knew that God would come to this world with mercy for those who desperately needed it, and forgiveness for the people who had fallen behind. They could have another chance; they could get up and go on again. Coming at Christmas was a God who would start all over again with those who wanted him to.

This is a tremendous message that Christmas brings of a God who comes down seeking to undo what people have done, seeking to find a way to forgive sin, seeking to break people out of their self-made prisons. That is a word for each one of us today.

We, too, have been those who have not always listened carefully to God. We know what he wants us to do, but we've not always been willing to do it. We know that we need to worship; we know that we need to give and serve, but we've not always been willing to do it. Because we have not, our lives are the losers. We suffer a loss of life, a loss of peace, a loss of joy because we have not really "feared the Lord."

The Christmas story is that we can start all over again; for those of us who wish it, Christ will forget the past, put it aside, and start with a new present and a new hope. Forgiveness is very possible.

I think the boy had it right. Someone was telling him that he'd been a bad boy, and therefore at Christmas, he was going to get a sock full of switches. (I heard that a lot when I was young.) But one boy told the other one, "No, that's not right. Christmas is a celebration of Christ's coming. He came to take all the switches out of the socks."

It may not be very theological, but I have a feeling it's very truthful. The sins that we have committed, the mistakes we have made—Jesus came to take them away, if we want him to.

3. He is a God who came to exalt the righteous.

All the way through Mary's song, there was an affirmation of victory, that God was a God who would honor Abraham and the promise he made. That promise was that if they trusted him and did his will, he would make out of them a great nation; they would be part of his kingdom.

What Mary was singing was that God would do that. Those who loved him and followed him would be the victors. It didn't seem like it, but this is what Mary said: "He has scattered the proud in the imagination of their hearts, he has put down the mighty from their thrones, . . . the rich he has sent empty away" (vv. 51-53). Now these were the ones who seemed to be on top of things: the rich, powerful kings, those who had money, those who had power, those who could snap their fingers and people would jump. They were the ones who seemed to be the victors; not some ragtag bunch of Jewish people singing about God coming, not poor and needy people who had little power and prestige, not them.

But Mary sang of the little people. He has "exalted those of low degree;/he has filled the hungry with good things" (vv. 52-53). In other words, Mary said that those who love the Lord will not be disappointed, will not be forgotten. They will share in his kingdom.

In our day it seems that those who seek to serve God do not seem to be the ones who are winning, but losing. Instead it seems that sometimes the people we idolize, the people we think have made it, are those who seem to be the God-neglecting. These people often tell us that what we need to do is live for pleasure—satisfy our desires—that's what life is all about. They seem to have everything they want, and at times we may find ourselves envying them.

Or we idolize a rock star, in and out of drugs, in and out of relationships with so many women, all the money in the world. Thousands upon thousands go to hear him sing. Sometimes down deep inside, we may envy a person like this.

We may idolize that powerful business executive who flies everywhere in his jet, meets with presidents of all countries, throws parties that make headlines, has so much power that it seems he can go anywhere and do anything he wants to. How we envy him and say that he has it made.

Who ever notices that person who may be living decently, trying to do what is right in his home and community; who's faithful to his family and his children; who is a member of his church and seeks to serve it faithfully; who seeks to care for the needy in his community; who puts in an honest day's work for what seems like an ever decreasing paycheck; who coaches Little League baseball simply because he loves children; who tries in every way that he can to make his bit of the world a better place to live in? He never makes the headlines; he never really gains much power, he just gets by paying the bills at the end of the month. Who notices him? Who idolizes him? Who sets him up as the epitome of how to live?

God does! God knows and notices, and God blesses those who in the way they can seek to follow him and to do his will in the places where they live. They may never be spectacular, but they are faithful. Therefore,

God will bless them with something that usually all those others we mentioned will not have; he will bless them with a sense of life, a sense of peace, a sense of purpose.

I think that if you look at all those others who seem to have it made— if you look in their eyes—you can see a sort of emptiness, a sort of boredom, a sort of unhappiness that betrays the feeling that somehow life has passed them by. Therefore, they go from place to place, from job to job, from relationship to relationship hoping maybe to find something that will bring them peace of mind and soul and spirit. For they are the hollow ones, in spite of their worldly success.

Sometimes you and I feel the emptiness, too. The only way the emptiness can ever be filled is if we seriously try to live the way that Christ lived before us. The truth is that life is a gift of God. He made it, gave it to us, and only when we live it by the rules and ways that he has set out will we get the most out of it.

Only when we give will we find. Only when we lose will we receive. Only when we love will we be loved. Only when we do it his way will we truly live. But if we do it his way, what we will discover in the midst of our lives is life, a sense of joy, a sense of hope, and a sense of peace. This is what he said at Christmas. When we live his way, we will be the victor.

A black theologian, Henry Mitchell, told of a time in his life as a child. It was the depression and his father was ill and could not work for three months. It was Christmas and they were sure that when Christmas day came for these little children there would be nothing under the Christmas tree for them. But they were surprised, for on Christmas there was a present for each one of the children: roller skates for him, he said.

They were surprised because their father had been sick. They watched as he got up and read this statement from Scripture, one which he said that he has never forgotten. "I have been young, and now am old; yet have I not seen the righteous forsaken, nor his seed begging bread" (Ps. 37:25, KJV).

"I have been young, and now am old; yet have I not seen the righteous forsaken, nor his seed begging bread." God will not disappoint us, that's what he was saying. If we struggle to live God's way, not only in the long run but in the short run, we will discover pieces and patches of joy and love and celebration that are worth everything. He will not leave us; he will exalt us.[3]

This Christmas, as you think of all the things that you have to do, I hope you're not groaning. I hope instead that you're happy over it. I always enjoy the Christmas season. It's my most favorite time of the year. I enjoy the music, I enjoy the parties, I enjoy the celebrations. I enjoy the worship. I enjoy them because to me it means that the Christ I have loves me.

This is what Christmas says: Christ comes again to look you in the eye and to say, "I love you." All the celebrating that we do at Christmas is our opportunity to look him back in the face and say, "We love you." God is trying to find you again. I hope this Christmas, you will make sure he does.

NOTES

1. Eugene Laubach, "The Baby and the Mad King," Sermons: Riverside Church, New York, New York, 1 Jan. 1978, p. 2.

2. Michael Daves, *Come with Faith* (New York: Abingdon Press, 1965), p. 28.

3. Henry H. Mitchell, "To Teach Them Diligently," *National Radio Pulpit* (July-Sept. 1978), p. 7.

ZECHARIAH'S SONG

What God Means

(Luke 1:67-79)

What does Christmas mean to you? That's a question that's been asked a lot of times these past few days. I'm sure you've heard it several times. What does Christmas mean to you? There are a lot of answers.

A businessman said that Christmas meant that his store would be busier than any other time of the year. That's why he liked Christmas. Christmas to him meant more sales. The teenager said that Christmas meant a good time because there were so many parties to go to, and she enjoyed it. Christmas to her was a fun time. The worker said that Christmas meant a bonus. He worked all year long, and now he would get a little extra money to live on, and he looked forward to that. And a child said that Christmas means Santa Claus coming to bring toys. Christmas meant presents to get.

Sometimes when I hear what Christmas means to some people, I am reminded of the company that gave a banquet in honor of one of its employees. All the preparations were made. The night came for the banquet and everyone was there—except the guest of honor. When they went around checking to find out what had happened they discovered, to their embarrassment, that nobody had invited him to come![1]

At Christmas, we remember that it is the celebration of the birth of Christ. But the problem with Christmas is that we can go through all the celebrations and not invite him to them. We must not do that. We must not have Christmas without Christ. We can't anyway. Christmas means the celebration of Christ. We can have a holiday, we can have celebrations, but we can never have Christmas unless Christ is there.

But what does Christmas mean? That's the question we need to answer. What does God mean to us through Christ at Christmas? Enter Zechariah, a man we don't usually associate with Christmas. But Zechariah, in Matthew and Luke, plays a very important part.

65

Zechariah was the father of John the Baptist. He had been made unable to speak because he had not believed the angel's message. When he learned of John the Baptist's birth and when he learned that Mary was going to have a child, suddenly he began to speak and prophesy and sing his song. It is a song that explains what Christmas was going to mean to them and, even now, to us.

What does Christmas mean? What did God want to do with it?

1. God means Christmas to save us from our lostness.

Zechariah was thankful that "he has visited and redeemed his people,/ and has raised up a horn of salvation for us" (vv. 68-69). Zechariah was talking about the fact that God was going to come and save them from their lostness, their misery. They needed it. Israel had rebelled against God, and they were now suffering the consequences of it. They were an oppressed people living under the feet of the Roman Empire. They were the sufferers who knew what it was to live in poverty and slavery. They were often the hopeless, for they had cried for God's help many times, and he had not come. Many were beginning to feel that he would never come.

But Zechariah knew that he was coming. There was a way out of their misery. Mary's baby would be born in Bethlehem and they would call his name Jesus, for he would save them from their sins. There was grace and love coming into the world and that meant a way out of the prisons they were in.

God meant to save them and he means to save us from our lostness. But we aren't the lost, are we? When we think of lostness, we usually think of some shabby character who's wasted his life and now lies in some gutter in some godforsaken place. That's what it means to be lost. We aren't the lost. Is that really true?

What does it mean to be lost? To be lost is to be empty inside and not be able to find anything in the world to do to stop it. We try to fill the void with some person, activity, pill, bottle or drug—anything in the world to numb the emptiness inside, to keep us from having to face our own inner vacuum.

To be lost is to come upon some crises in life and discover that we have no resources with which to face them. We're going under, as it were, for the last time and there is no way we feel we can stay afloat.

To be lost is to feel lonely and unloved, to feel that no one can ever care about you, not even God.

To be lost is to live for self, to think that all that matters is what you want and what you are. It is to live for pleasure that satisfies your desires. It is to use people, not to love them. It is to play God by wanting only you to be king of your life.

To be lost is to be caught by guilt that will not go away. It causes you to toss and turn in the night. It haunts you down the steps of your days. You have guilt and it's frightening, but you can't get rid of it.

To be lost is to be full of hatred, to be full of unforgiveness, to be full of indifference to other people's needs.

Do we know what it is to be lost? Have we ever tasted some of those empty feelings? To be lost is to feel hopeless. Some of us know it. We're caught in the misery, loneliness, and pain of life and there seems to be no way out.

Then the music of Christmas breaks forth: "Joy to the world, the Lord is come!" There is a way out of your lostness—Jesus Christ! He has come with his forgiveness for our sins. He has come with his love for our feeling of unloveliness. He has come with his grace to help us handle the crises of life. He has come to give us meaning and purpose in life. He has come to set us free from that which would destroy us. That's what he meant by Christmas. To come down to the world to a people who felt that they were godforsaken and to find them and to bring them home. That's what he means to do for you—if you let him.

In the Civil War, many soldiers were imprisoned in Nashville. A lady appeared at the gate of the prison and said that she needed to see her teenage son, that he shouldn't be in there and that the commandant said she could get her son. She went into that prison and said, "I have teenage clothes for somebody. I haven't a son, but I can free one of you." So they got together and chose a captain. He got into the clothes, and she took him by the arm and walked past the guards and said, "Come, we've got some plowing to do." Past the guards they went, out of the prison to freedom.[2]

In a sense, God has walked into our prisons and said, "I have got a way out for you. It's forgiveness; it's love; it's service and if you will don these clothes, I will set you free." Every one of us who puts them on—every one of us who puts our trust in him—will find Christmas meaningful because we will be saved from that lostness that will choke out our lives. Do you need it? You can have it. Christ has come.

2. God means Christmas to give us meaning by using us in his work.

There is an interesting phrase in this song. Zechariah gave thanks because they "might serve him without fear" (v. 73). What does that mean? There are two possible meanings.

One is without fear of harm from others. To serve God got them in trouble sometimes with the Romans. They were often persecuted for it; they were criticized for it, told they were crazy. Now they wouldn't be bothered.

The other possible meaning is this—the one I like best: The Jews had been serving God with timidity, not really sure that serving him would do any good. They had come to believe that maybe they were hopeless in trying to serve him. So their service to God lacked the fire and dedication they ought to have. Now Zechariah knew that he was coming, that his faith was not in vain. So Zechariah said they could serve him without fear or timidity, but with boldness because he knew it was true. What they did for God mattered. Service in his work was worthwhile. Zechariah knew that his own life had meaning, that God needed him, and that what he did for God would never be forgotten.

God means to use us. That's one reason he comes at Christmas, to seek us out to say, "I need you in my service. Give yourself to me and let me use you." Christmas was a time when God renewed his promise to bless us through Christ. Christmas ought to be a time on our part when we renew our promises to serve him. All of us have made promises to God, have we not? When we came down the aisle of our church, we made a commitment to Christ, that we wanted to follow him. That commitment contains a promise to try to serve him to the best of our ability. We who follow Him made that promise. How well have we kept it?

Many of you have stood across the front of this sanctuary with little children cradled in your arms. You came for what we call a "Parent-Child Dedication Service," and you dedicated your child to God and promised to bring that child up in the nurture of the Lord, to make your homes Christian, to involve your children in the church. Have you kept that promise?

Many have promised me that they were going to join the church because they know that they need to be involved in it, to be identified with a community of faith, to make their life count for something, somewhere. They promised to join the church, but they have not done it yet. Some have promised to accept Christ as Savior and Lord, but have not done it yet. Some have promised to serve Christ, to sing in the choir, to teach in Sunday School, to serve on committees, to be a witness, to visit.

All the promises I have heard—all the promises you have made—have you kept them? When we made our promises we meant them, I know that. We were sincere. We started out with good intentions. But we quickly discovered that serving God was hard work. It took a lot of time. Often it was frustrating when nothing much seemed to be accomplished by what we did. Trying to serve God brought criticism. With all of these things falling upon us and all of the many activities calling for our time, we found it easy to let our promise slide.

Listen! God needs you still! God wants to use you still! He has work for you to do, and you must give your life to him. If you will involve yourself in his work, you will discover the joy that Christmas is about. You will find out that you are here to serve, to give. Only when we serve God and others will life begin to come alive for us the way it should.

Christmas can be a time to renew our commitments to serve him. When Langley was governor of North Dakota, he was asked to have a dinner for a noted Christian who was coming to Bismarck to speak at a YMCA meeting. This man was known worldwide for the tremendous work that he had done. The governor was looking forward to meeting this person that had done so much and been so vital to the work of Christian ministry.

When the governor came home to dinner and saw him, he was shocked. Standing before him was a man who was not quite five feet tall. A look of surprise and disgust came over the governor's face. The man seemed to notice the look of surprise and disgust on the governor's face and said to him, "Governor, isn't it amazing what God can use?"[3]

It is. It's amazing that God can use me. It's amazing that God can use you, but he can. I hope this Christmas we will renew the promises we have made to him and keep them.

3. God means to bring us home by giving us encouragement.

Zechariah's song ended on a very hopeful note. He said that this one who would come would "give light to those who sit in darkness and in the shadow of death,/to guide our feet in the way of peace" (v. 79). They were a people who sat in darkness with little hope, but now hope was breaking into the world. Even in the face of death, there was hope, Zechariah said. God had come in Christ to be with them. Therefore, the darkness would not be the conqueror, life would. They could endure, they could go on, and they did go on.

Eventually that baby grew up to draw around him a rag-tag group of disciples who seemed so small, so tiny. But out they went into the world and turned it upside down. The darkness that surrounded Bethlehem at Christmas time has given way to the light of the joy that we sing because the Lord has come.

A submarine crew's last words as it was sinking, tapped through the walls to those trying to save it, were, "Is there any hope?" That's a desperate question. That's an eternal question. It's being asked over and over again today. In the face of all of the overwhelming problems we see daily people ask, "Is there any hope?"

Many answer, "No. No hope." Some tell us that things are just going to get worse and worse and there is nothing we can do about it. Others tell us that it is inevitable that we are going to have a nuclear war. Others say you can't change things because people can't be changed. To all of these statements and all of the prophets of doom, Christmas comes with this message to say, "Oh, who said?" It's an old adage that you can't teach an old dog new tricks. That is a lie. If that were true, then there is no need to preach the gospel at all. The heart of the gospel is that anybody can be changed with the help of God. You can change, none of you have to stay the way you are. If you want to change the way you live and the way you feel, trust Christ and depend on him to help you, and he'll do it. Not only will Christ change you, if you let him; but he will use you to change the world.

Things don't have to stay the way they are, things can be better because Christ is with us and there is hope let loose in the world. You can make a difference. The church can! Maybe we can bring more light to the darkness.

There's a psychiatrist in New York City named John Rosen who works with catatonics. He breaks the precedent of doctors remaining separate and aloof from their patients. He moves into the ward with them. He places his bed among their beds. He lives the life they must live. Day to day, he shares it. He loves them. If they don't talk, he doesn't talk either. It's as if he understands what's happening. He's just there, and that communicates something to them that they haven't heard in years— somebody understands.

But then he does something else. He puts his arms around them and hugs them. This highly-skilled, highly-paid physician who is like God to the patient, who sets the limits on their lives, holds these unattractive, unlovable, sometimes out of control persons and loves them back into life. Often, when they speak, the first words they say are thank you.

The difference in the life of many was one person who cared. The difference between hopelessness and hope for many people dwelling in this world and near us is one person who cares. Christ has come to make a difference to us. The power that he has given us is the power to go out into this world and to change it. It is always available because Christ is always available. Hope—it will never die because he is here!

So if you hear the question again, and you probably will, "What does Christmas mean to you?," I hope that you will be able to tell them. I hope that you will tell them Christmas means that we have been saved from our lostness and that Christ has come to set us free. I hope you'll be able to say that Christmas means that you have meaning in your life because Christ has come to use you. I hope you'll be able to say that Christmas means hope because Christ has come to dwell with us in the midst of the darkness, therefore light will always shine. What I hope you will tell people who ask you is that Christmas means that Christ is alive within you. When all is said and done, that's what Christmas means.

She was old now, her body aching from arthritis, almost an invalid; and she lived in a rundown section in a rundown room in Richmond near the state penitentiary. But there was one thing about her that one would not forget. She was a singer, and whenever people went to visit her she was always listening to music. She always wanted guests to sing a song with her. That's unusual. We don't run into many people, at any age, who love to sing with us. But that was the way her life was: radiant, full of joy, always a song. I remember her pastor saying at her funeral, "Mrs. Jacobs always had a song in her heart, and the reason she always had a song in her heart was because Christ was there to help her sing it."

That's what Christmas means; the music never stops because Christ is there to help us keep on singing. We can always sing because Christ has come!

NOTES

1. Lowell Atkinson, "Winter Without Christmas," *Pulpit Digest*, Dec. 1958, p. 71.
2. *Pulpit Resource*, (Jan.-Mar. 1981), p. 7.
3. Ibid., p. 22.
4. *Pulpit Resource*, (Oct.-Dec. 1980), p. 43.

THE ANGEL'S SONG

The Dream We Covet

(Luke 2:13-14)

Sometime during this Christmas this question will be asked, possibly by you. It may be as you sit by the fire with the ones you love. It may be as you celebrate a joyful moment. It may be as you sit and contemplate all that Christmas means to you. Then the question comes: Why can't it be like this always? Why can't Christmas last all year long? For there is something about the Christmas spirit that strikes a responsive chord in us and causes us to think about the fact that the world could be better than it is.

Christmas is a time for dreamers to dream about a world that is not, but can be. At one time, most of us were dreamers. When we were young we were going to change the world, remember? We were going to dash out into it and right all the existing wrongs. Out we went with good intentions, but we bumped into a harsh reality. The world is not easy to change and often people don't want to change. Because of that, we began to see our dreams fade into the background. They were impossible dreams anyway, weren't they? So we got down to the business of trying to survive in this world.

But Christmas keeps coming back. Christmas keeps coming to try to stir up the forgotten ashes and embers of those dreams. Christmas causes us, if just for a moment, to wonder: Why can't we have a world where peace and love and joy are the way it is? Still, all the time we dream; inside of our minds lies the thought that it's impossible.

The angels were wrong, weren't they? For they came bursting onto the scene crying out, "Glory to God in the highest, and on earth peace, good will toward men" (v. 14, KJV). We say, "What a dream!" Oh, that it could be! How we would love a world like that! This is the dream we covet: peace on earth, goodwill toward men. But can it ever be? Was Christmas wrong? Was the song of the angels a pipe dream, or can it really be?

73

1. It's a dream about peace on earth.

When Christ was born, there was peace on earth in the sense that no wars were being fought within the Roman Empire, which included most of the known world. Rome was in charge. We see that because Mary and Joseph went to Bethlehem to register for taxes. There wasn't anything they could do about it.

There was no war outwardly, but inwardly within the heart of people there burned violence, mistrust, and hatred of their Roman conquerors. While no war was being fought, the seeds of it were certainly there. Into the midst of that unhealthy, tense atmosphere, the angels sang of peace on earth and others said it couldn't be. But they sang it because, since Christ was born in Bethlehem, there could be peace on earth.

If there is one thing this world needs, it's peace. We certainly don't have it. There is trouble all over the world. Place your finger almost anywhere on a world map and you will find trouble there. Our world lives on the brink of war. Even today, we talk almost matter-of-factly about a limited nuclear war. The prophets of old warned against crying out, "'Peace, peace,' when there is no peace" (Jer. 6:14). We don't have to worry about that today. Nobody is crying peace. We know that it is not here.

Yet we want it. In any survey taken that asks people what they want most, the number one answer is usually peace. We dream of it, we sing about it at Christmas, but do we think it's possible? Are we doing anything to see that the dream comes true?

Pablo Casals died at the age of ninety-six. He was one of the world's great musicians. He was also a man dedicated to peace. A native of Spain, he loved his country dearly, but when Franco came to power with his repressive government, he left Spain. He never would play a musical concert in any country run by a tyrannical dictator. He believed that music was a universal language and he would play his music seeking to talk about the joy and love of it in the hope that by the playing of music, people would learn to live together. He said, "I have given everything I know how to give to peace. It may not be much, but at least I have given what I could for this sacred ideal."[1]

We who sing for peace at Christmas, do we give anything to see it come to pass? Have we given up on peace? Do we still believe it's possible? Sometimes, to cry out for peace in our world seems to be like a lone voice crying in the wilderness. To cry out for peace will not meet with responsive ears. To call for us to take the risks for peace will not always be met with affirmative nods. To be those who try to be peacemakers is not always popular work. But the alternative to peace is insanity. We need to dream of peace.

My dream is symbolized in a story that Basil Matthews told as he visited the Middle East. He was sitting by a brook, and he heard some beautiful music being piped. The music was coming from a homemade flute that he heard a shepherd boy playing. As the boy got closer, he came to him and showed him the flute.

To Matthew's surprise, the flute was made out of the barrel of a rifle. Evidently the boy had found it left from one of the many battles that had been fought in those areas. He had taken it, hollowed it out, filed it down and cut holes in it so that it could produce beautiful sounds. With that flute made from a gun barrel, he brought beautiful music to his neighbors and even to strangers.[2]

That's the hope that, somehow in what we try to do, we can take the gun barrels of war and make them into instruments of music for peace. The swords can be beaten to plowshares.

2. They dreamed of goodwill toward men with whom God is well pleased.

There wasn't much goodwill in those days. Many, like the Romans, didn't believe in God. Many, like some Jewish people, didn't take him seriously. As a result, there was ill will among the people. They mistrusted one another, were suspicious of one another, hated one another. Then the angels sang "good will toward men," and the Jews said, "You've got to be kidding. Goodwill toward the Samaritans? Goodwill toward the Romans? Goodwill toward the Greeks? Not on your life!" But the angel sang on: "Good will toward men" because Christ is born!

We need goodwill among people today. Wouldn't it be nice if we could have a brotherhood of humanity where we treated each other with dignity and respect, regardless of color of skin or origin of birth or place on an economic ladder? Wouldn't it be nice if we could get along with one another? We don't seem to be able to treat each other well.

An editorial told about a number of handgun deaths in 1980 across the world. In every country around the world there were less than one hundred handgun deaths—except the United States. In the United States, there were over ten thousand. We are violent. We do not get along. We treat each other harshly.

Marriage is now undergoing 51 percent divorce rates. Some young people coming to be married want the words "till death do us part" taken out of their marriage ceremony. They want instead "till love dies," as if they know that when they get married it will probably not last.

At Christmas, for just a moment, we begin to feel closer to one another. We treat the poor a little bit better, trying to take care of their needs. We are even friendlier towards our neighbors and a lot of times we even get along better in our homes. Maybe we can get along.

Whenever I think of brotherhood at Christmas, I cannot forget that experience I had as a teenager. It was Christmas Eve and I was helping the pastor take some Christmas baskets to needy families in our area. I remember vividly taking baskets to one black family. The husband was paralyzed, the mother had four children. They were needy.

We began bringing in some of these baskets and a boy, about four or five years of age, was confused by all of these strange people entering his home. He asked his mother, "Who are these people?" She explained to him, "They are the people from the Baptist church, and they are bringing us these Christmas baskets." As all boys seem to have to do at that age, he asked that eternal question, "Why?" The mother paused for a few moments and then came up with an answer: "Why? Because they love us." That little boy came to me, I guess because I was eavesdropping and I was the closest one around, tugged at my shirt, looked up at me out of those big eyes and said, "Mister, do you love me?"

How would you answer that? For you see, because we have answered no so many times we do not have goodwill toward people. What Christmas comes down to tell us is that God wants us to say yes to all those who ask us the question, "Do you love me?" Because of Christ we can. Do you think it's impossible? Do you think we are stupid to dream that dream and sing that song of goodwill toward men? Can we get along?

3. It's a dream of total commitment to God.

Here is the key to the angel's song: Glory to God in the highest. That meant that all worship and honor went to him; that meant that everybody needed to love him. Everybody needed to worship him. Everybody needed to serve him. If that happened—glory was given to

God in the highest—then peace on earth, goodwill towards men could happen.

That's the secret! The secret is not that you and I on our own will go out into this world and by some miraculous superhuman effort bring peace on earth and goodwill toward all people. The secret is that this God who has come in Christ will bring peace if we will let him use us. But can it be? We dream of it. If only everybody would love God, what a nice world that would be! But in order for that to happen *we* have got to give glory to God, and that means you and I have got to take God seriously. You and I have got to believe his way of life. You and I have got to put him first in our lives.

The danger of Christmas is that we will go on worshiping the baby Jesus. Babies are pretty. But Jesus grew up and looked at us from a cross and said, "Follow me. Take up your cross daily. Leave it all behind and follow me" (Author's translation). Are we willing to worship that Christ? For until we are, the dream is impossible.

I have seen it happen many times. A boy was running up and down through an arcade where they have all these bubble gum machines. The boy went from one bubble gum machine to the other, turning the slots, hoping by some magic that there was a piece of bubble gum that may come out of it. He had no coin to put into it, but he kept clicking every one of them hoping that maybe some way he would get some bubble gum.

Often, we have been going through life turning the switches hoping by some magic we may find peace on earth and goodwill to all people. But we have to be willing to pay the price: your life and mine given honestly and seriously to Christ. Until God gets the glory, we don't get what we need.

Can Christmas last always? Maybe it can. Maybe it can last for us if we would try to live day by day by giving glory to God and seeking his dream.

There was a B movie on TV entitled *Hard Times Texas*. It was about a town named Hard Times that really had them. They had the town going for a while, but the town drunk burned everything down one night. After that, everybody moved away except the sheriff. The old sheriff would stand at the city limits and whenever somebody would come by he would stop them and say, "I've got a dream. We can rebuild this city. Will you help me?"

He did that over and over again until finally, he got enough people to rebuild the city. When they did, all of the other people came back including the town drunk who turned around and burned everything down again. Everybody left again, and as the movie ends you see the old sheriff standing by the city limits, stopping somebody by saying, "I have a dream, we can rebuild this city if you help me."[3]

What you and I need to do is to stand in this world, grab people and say, "Hey, we've got a dream. We can build a world where there's peace on earth and goodwill toward men. It can be done. Will you help us?" Maybe if we stay at it long enough and hard enough, always giving the glory to God, it might happen! You see, the dream is God's dream and that dream *will* come true. If we begin giving the glory to God, maybe we can help it come true a little bit sooner.

NOTES

1. *Pulpit Resource* (July-Sept. 1978), p. 34.

2. Benjamin P. Browne, *Illustrations for Preaching* (Nashville: Broadman Press, 1977), pp. 92-93.

3. Edwin Muller, "Response to New Life—A View From Prison," Sermon: Riverside Church, New York, New York, 13 Jan. 1974, pp. 9-10.

CHRIST'S SONG

A Love for All Seasons

(Christmas Eve Communion)

Every year we don't think we are going to make it. We get so caught up in the Christmas celebration with all of the things that we have to do and it gets us so tired. We get tired of the traffic and tired of the crowds, tired of wrapping presents, tired of cooking, tired of going to this party and that, even tired of going to church. We get tired and don't think we're going to make it.

But we always do. Somehow miraculously, we get done all that needs to be done. We have come together tonight to try to remember why. On an African safari one day, the natives did not get up to carry the luggage. When asked why not, they said that they needed time for their "souls to catch up with their bodies."

That's why we need these moments, to give time for our souls to catch up with our bodies, to try to get everything in proper perspective. What I want us to remember is the song that Christ sang at Christmas. Now we know that Christ has something to do with Christmas. We are warned, "Don't take Christ out of Christmas." But that's not our danger because we know that he is the reason we celebrate it. Our danger is that we can get so busy with preparations for it that unconsciously, we might nudge him to the edges of our Christmas celebration and miss the true significance of what Christmas is about. It is about a love that's for all seasons, a love that meets all of our needs forever. It's a song in three parts.

1. The first stanza begins with a birth.

A baby was born in Bethlehem in a stable. There wasn't anything unusual about that. It had probably happened before; it probably happened again. So why all the fuss? Why shepherds and Wise Men and angels and stars? What was the big deal about that baby's birth? The big deal had to do with *who* he was.

79

For a long time the people had begun to believe that God had forsaken them. It had been over two hundred years now since they had heard a prophet from God. Surely they had disobeyed him, but they had done that in the past and God had always come back and started over with them. But now, like a child playing hide and seek who hides and no one looks for him, they began to wonder if God was still looking for them. Had he forgotten? Had he given up? In the midst of their poverty and their oppression and their suffering, they wondered if God had forgotten them.

Then a baby cried, shepherds and Wise Men worshiped, angels sang, a star shone bright, and the good news went out. God had not forgotten! He remembered! He came to love them, to save them, to help them. He came to be where they were!

Christmas is a reminder that God has come to be where we are. Into the midst of all of our lives, our confusion, our suffering, the trouble of this world, God has come to pitch his tent right next to us. He has come to look us, as it were, in the face to say, "I know you. I know who you are and what you need. I have not forgotten you."

Under the Christmas tree at your house, there are presents with names on them. As an adult, just as when I was a child, I look at those presents underneath the tree to see if there's a tag with my name on it, a gift just for me. One Christmas Eve, a young man and his girl friend sat underneath the tree. He reached in and pulled out a present and gave it to her. It had her name on it. Nervously, she opened the package and saw a beautiful diamond ring. As she put it on her finger, he said, "I love you, and I will love you forever." It was a special, special gift.[1]

At Christmas God has sent us a gift, wrapped with our names on it, addressed just to you or to me. As we open it, it is Christ. As I see him, the angels sing what God wants me to know. "I love you and I will love you forever." That's a song worth hearing. With shepherds and Wise Men, we should join together in worshiping this precious Christmas gift.

2. The second stanza is a song about a death.

Babies do grow up. Christ left that cradle and became a man. As he went about doing God's will, he got into trouble with the religious leaders. They would not fellowship with sinners: he ate with them. They were judgmental of sinners: he forgave them. They lived hypocritically, playing at religion: Christ was the man who had integrity of word and deed. He was what he said. They loved only a few: he loved them all.

They asked for a cheap price to pay: keeping the rules. He came calling for total commitment of life: it was the only way to live.

It's no wonder that, finally, a cross had to be lifted up. This tiny baby boy who had grown up to be the man Jesus had to be crucified. He was too good to live. If they let him alone they would have to change and they did not want that. All along he told them that he knew what they needed for life: "Follow my way. Do it my way and you will have life abundant." They did not want to follow. Instead they nailed the nails through his hands and hung him there and turned and walked away.

When Christ died on that hill (which was a garbage dump), it was his way of telling us how much he understood us. He had come to live in our shoes and to face what we face. There is nothing in the world that you and I can face that Christ has not already faced himself. Suffering? He knows that. He hung from a cross and knew the physical and the mental suffering of that. Loneliness and rejection? He knows that, too. The crowds turned away from him; his own disciples left him, and on the cross he felt forsaken by God. He was alone.

Doubt? He wrestled with it asking the Father to remove the cross. Misunderstanding? He was really misunderstood not only by the crowds and his disciples, but by his own family who thought he was crazy. And death? He faced it, too. Christ comes to look us in the face to say, "Look, I know the way to live; and if you follow me, I will give it to you." And we tell him, "But look, it's too tough, too difficult; it hurts. We run into too many problems. You don't understand." He turns and says, "But I do understand. I was there. I walked through it. I faced it. I know how to come through it because I did it. If you trust me, I will help you come through it too. I understand."

At times we may wonder if there is a God who does understand us. But God is not a God living in some far away heaven oblivious to what goes on down here where we dwell. He is a God who understands because he faced it all even to the point of throwing himself on a cross to help us know how much he did understand.

In Dostoevski's *The House of Death*, it was Christmas Day in a Siberian prison camp. The prisoners were at one end of the village and at the other end of the village was a cathedral high on a hill. They could hear the Christmas bells on that Christmas morning. As they looked through the bars on their windows, they saw all of the peasants making their way to the cathedral. How they wished that somehow they could be there, too. But there was no way, for they were cut off from humanity. "God is not here with us," they said. After the celebration in the cathedral was over, the priest came to the prison camp and set up a crude altar and started to celebrate Christ's mass. One of the convicts cried out, "Now God is here with us." The priest said, "You don't understand. God is always here with you. He just goes to the cathedral on special occasions. But He is always here with you."[2]

That's where that baby who came chose to dwell, in the midst of human suffering, human hurt, human need. He dwells where we are. We can know that each step of the way we go, there is a God who understands the pain and the struggles as well as the joy. He so loved us that he went through it all himself so we would know we are understood. Let us always thank him for that.

3. Stanza three is a song about resurrection!

You know that if Christ had not been raised from the dead, we would not have Christmas to celebrate. If he had not been raised, he would have just been another good man who died, a memory but not a Savior. Christmas is joy to us because Christ grew up to be the Savior who conquered all that would defeat us. He conquered suffering. We don't understand suffering but how we detest it. We wonder how we can get through it. But he did. He is a Christ who conquered sin. Sin is so powerful; it drags us down and destroys us. It can even cause us to crucify the Son of God. But he defeated that. And death! We don't like to think of that. It seems to be so final. We all have a date with death but how we fear it. But he conquered that!

This is the joy of Christmas: Easter. We can't have Christmas without Easter. Easter and now Christmas mean that those who face suffering, who face difficulty, who are struggling under insurmountable burdens have a Savior that knows the way to help us triumph over it. Easter and now Christmas mean that in our struggle with sin, there is forgiveness for our failures. There is strength and courage to get up and try again. Easter and now Christmas mean that death is not our end but a door that leads to that which is beyond. What is beyond we do not know. *Who* is beyond we do know. This Christ who came is there. He is a Christ who sets us free. Nothing can stop us because nothing could stop him.

There was a mongoloid boy named Philip in a third grade class in Sunday School. He couldn't keep up too well, seemed out of place. He was different and the other boys teased him, ridiculed him, and gave him the cold shoulder. One Easter, the teacher brought those big plastic eggs and gave one to each of these boys and said, "I want you to go outside and find something in the yard that symbolizes what Easter means to you." They went out, Philip included, and brought all of the eggs back and put them on the table and began to open each one. One had a flower in it and everybody "ooed" and "ahed." Another opened it and a little butterfly flew out.

One opened his and it held a rock. Somebody yelled, "How stupid, a rock!" The boy spoke up, "I knew that you were going to have flowers and butterflies and pretty things. I put in a rock because I want to be different. I am different. That is the good news of Easter to me; I am a unique, special individual." The teacher smiled at such brilliance from a little boy.

Then they opened another one and it was empty. Nothing in it. The boys began to say, "Somebody didn't play fair. That's not right. Somebody didn't do what they were supposed to do." The teacher felt little Philip tugging at his shirt. Philip said, with eyes wide open, "It's mine. It's mine. It's empty because the tomb is empty! The tomb is empty." Somehow Philip wasn't different any more. Somehow Philip was in because here was a boy that knew the truth. Easter meant that Christ was alive. Now Christmas means the same truth, Christ is alive![3]

That's what it all means: Christ, now and forever! If we don't remember that and worship him, then no matter what tomorrow brings it will not be enough. I hope that you have remembered. We need to hear this in the world in which we live. It's a world that speaks not so much of Christ, not so much of hope, not so much of love, but we know better because Christ is here.

Dorothy Stott Shaw wrote of the angels' song on that night:

Perhaps it will be longer than we thought
    Between the fair and final "Peace on Earth,"
And the great first "Fear Not!"
    But in between there are good tidings still,
And there are angels telling this tonight.

Listen, oh listen! We are not alone!
    Rising above our weeping and our wars
Confident great voices, not our own
    Cry joy, cry peace, cry courage to the stars.

The way is plain, the destination sure,
    The end is peace, we need not be dismayed
For there are angels saying, "We shall endure
    And not to be afraid!"[4]

NOTES

1. William Ribbens, "Jesus Came to Be a Saviour" Unpublished Sermon: Grace Reformed Church, Burke, Virginia, 2 Dec. 1979, pp. 3-4.

2. Colbert Cartwright, "A Time for Pondering," (*Pulpit Digest*, Nov.-Dec. 1980), pp. 53-54.

3. Craig Biddle III, "The Empty Tomb," *Master Sermons*, April 1980, pp. 178-180.

4. Dorothy Stott Shaw, *Christmas Poems* (Colorado Springs, Colorado: Out West Printers, 1973), p. 21.

Catching Christmas

(Luke 2:25-35)

The question is often asked, "What did you get for Christmas?" Happy voices excitedly rattle off a list of things. At this time of year I am reminded of a Dennis the Menace cartoon. He was surrounded by a mountain of packages that he had opened. He looked at his parents and asked, "Is that all?" For several years he wanted a horse, but he was always disappointed because he never got it. Therefore, in spite of all the many things he did get, Christmas was always a disappointment to him. In a sense, he felt let down by Christmas.

Even though we do get the things we want for Christmas, there usually is a letdown that follows. It is called the "post-Christmas blues." We prepare so much for Christmas, get so excited about it, that we reach a high emotional peak and then "boom," it's all over so fast. We seem to tumble down emotionally. Like Dennis, we can stand in the midst of our things and ask, "Is that all? Is there anything more to it? Now what?"

This could have been the reaction of Mary and Joseph. The birth of their firstborn was an exciting moment with shepherds and a star and angels. What a special moment! But that night passed. The shepherds went back to work; the star disappeared; the angels quit singing. Now what? What would they do to keep that moment alive? What would they do to catch Christmas? For that is our question, too. How can we catch Christmas so that it becomes a continuous part of us? How can the deep meaning of Christ's birth and presence with us stay alive all year long?

In our Scriptures, Mary and Joseph took Jesus to the Temple to make a sacrifice to God and to thank him for the birth of the child. In the Temple was an old man named Simeon. God had promised him that he would see the Messiah before he died. When he saw the child, he knew he was the Promised One. He broke out in song and his song is one of the precious hymns of the faith. It is called "Nunc Dimittis." In it he told

85

of the meaning of Christ's coming. In it there are some hints as to how we can catch Christmas and keep its meaning alive.

1. To catch Christmas, we must seek to share it.

Simeon saw that Christ was to be the Savior of all the world. He was to be the "salvation which thou hast prepared in the presence of all peoples, a light for revelation to the Gentiles, and for glory to thy people Israel" (vv. 30-32). Gentiles were included; no one would be left out. Simeon sang that song for he knew the significance of Christ's coming. He was for all. Everyone had hope because Christ was born.

Now we know that. We know that Christ came to be the Savior of all people. He has saved us and brought us life. But many don't know. For many, the Christmas celebration centers only in parties and Christmas bonuses and family gatherings. But that is all. That's why many suffer from the post-Christmas blues, many commit suicide or get lost in alcoholic binges during Christmas. They do not know the hope and joy and love of Christmas because they do not know the Christ. They need to know. They have not heard the good news, and they must be told. We can be the tellers.

One way to catch Christmas and keep it alive is to share the good news of Christmas all year round, to be witnesses to the truth that unto us is born "a Savior, who is Christ the Lord" (v. 11). Others need to hear about the forgiveness Christ offers, of the grace he brings for our needs, of love he has for all. The telling of it keeps the meaning alive for us. When somebody hears and believes, the joy of that moment can never be put into mere human words.

Bill Rittinghouse wrote of an experience that he had that was published in the *Baptist Record*. In this experience, he was driving in Kansas and passed a station wagon that had luggage on top of it. One of the pieces of luggage fell off. The station wagon went on because the driver didn't know the luggage had fallen off. Some people picked it up and tried to find out whose it was. They opened it and the only clue to the owner's identity was a white box with a rubber band around it that had a twenty dollar gold piece between two layers of cotton. On one side of the gold piece were the words, "Twenty years loyal and faithful service." On the other side it read, "Presented to Otis Sampson by Northwestern States Portland Cement Company."

Rittinghouse wrote seventy-five cities in the Northwest seeking to find this particular person. Finally, he got a letter back from one of them that said that Sampson had formerly been employed but had recently retired. He wrote Mr. Sampson and told him how he found the suitcase and got an immediate reply. The man told him to dispose of the suitcase and all of the contents except for the gold piece; for, he said, "That's my most precious possession."

Rittinghouse answered his letter and enclosed the gold piece, but he also took the opportunity to tell him of his most precious possession. He told him how precious his family was to him, how precious life was because God had brought him safely home after World War II when he had been a prisoner of war in Romania. But, he said, "While these things are extremely precious to me, my most precious possession is Jesus Christ my Lord and Savior." He mailed the letter with a stamp on the outside and a prayer on the inside.

About a year later at Christmas, Rittinghouse received a box. Inside was a little white box with the same twenty dollar gold piece in it with an attached letter. Part of it read, "Last Sunday, my wife and I were baptized in the little church here in Colorado. We want you to have the gold piece to carry with you at all times. We are two old people. I am seventy-four years old, my wife is seventy-two. You were the first one to tell us of Jesus Christ. Now he is our most precious possession."[1]

You may think it's hard to believe that somebody that old had never heard of Jesus Christ before, but that is the way it is. Many have not. And the joy we have is being able to tell them. Imagine the joy in the life of Bill Rittinghouse when he realized that his testimony had been the means through which two people had found the good news to be true.

To catch Christmas, let us tell the good news. If someone hears, then the joy that we will feel will be the never-ending joy of Christmas.

2. To catch Christmas, we must seek to live it daily.

Simeon sang of a Christ who would bring out the best or the worst in people. Many would rise as they trusted him and followed him, many would fall as they rejected him and walked away. "Thoughts out of many hearts may be revealed" (v. 35). In other words, what people believed would be known, what they trusted would be seen. Would it be Christ or not? The answer to that would result in whether they rose or fell, had life or lost it.

For us that means that if we want to catch Christmas and keep it alive we must make a serious attempt to live for the Christ who came, to follow him in every way we can. We must be those who strive to be peacemakers, who seek to bring goodwill between persons, who seek to love. At Christmas, we do find people more willing to serve, more willing to do what needs to be done. We all seem to feel a little bit more closer to Christ at Christmas, more thankful for what he has done, more willing to give. But can we keep that spirit alive all year long? That's the question. It won't be easy. We have to stay with it, make the commitment day by day to put into practice all that we say we believe. We must stay with it.

There was a ball player who was sent down from the big leagues to a farm team. He was upset. He was a pitcher. He didn't want to go to the farm team. So instead of going north to the farm team, he turned south saying to his wife, "I am going to Louisiana. I'm not going to that farm team." His wife was quite surprised by this turn of events, but she knew that it wasn't the time to argue. She kept encouraging him saying such things as, "You are great, you really can make it, you have what it takes." But it seemed to do no good.

Later they stopped at a gas station and she said, "Honey, it is always going to bother me to think that you ran away, and I will never know whether you could have made it in the big leagues or not." He looked at her and said, "What's that you say?" She knew then that she had reached him. When they left the gas station, he turned north and went to the farm team.

That year he worked hard. The next year he was back in the big league. By 1979 he had helped his team win two world championships. He was declared pitcher of the year by the *Sporting News*. He won the Cy Young Award, emblematic of the best pitcher in the American League. His name is Ron Guidry. He would have missed all of that success; he would have lost all of the joy he discovered from those accomplishments if he had continued to run away. It was only when he decided to stay with it, to endure, that was it possible for him to know the joy.[2]

In the Christian life, in order for us to know the joy of Christian service, in order to know the benefits of what Christ has brought, we've got to live it day by day. Until we stay with it and try honestly to do his will in our daily lives, we will never really know what he has to give us. Christmas will die unless we seek to live it day by day.

3. To catch Christmas, we must be willing to pay the price that's asked of us.

Here was the hard word that Simeon sang to Mary: "A sword will pierce through your own soul" (v. 35). He told Mary that to be the mother of Christ would be costly. It would bring her pain and suffering and he was right. It brought pain when Christ left home to become an itinerant preacher. It brought her pain when she wondered if he might be crazy and begged him to come home, but he would not do it. It brought her pain when she stood at the foot of the cross and watched her son being crucified like a common criminal. Mary knew the pain of being his mother. But she stayed with it. She was willing to make that commitment to it. She knew the pain, but she would also know the joy.

To follow Christ, there is a price tag. It is a life totally committed to his way. If we want to know the joy and love of Christmas always, we must be willing to pay the price the Wise Men and shepherds paid. We must be willing to worship Christ giving him what we are. There is a price for you and a price for the church. Will we be willing to pay it?

For young people, the price is saying no to drugs and alcohol while others are saying yes, and that's hard to do. It will cause you to lose some popularity and maybe some friends. The question you will have to answer is: "Is Christ worth it?"

For adults, it means to be honest in business when others are not. It is to treat all people fairly when others are prejudiced. It is to talk of peace when others talk of war. It's to be faithful to marriage when others feel it is square to do so. The question that you will have to decide is this: "Is Christ worth it?"

For the church, it means doing work that needs to be done: singers in the choir, teachers in the Sunday School, workers in the nursery, committee workers. It will take time, and it will be inconvenient at times. It will not always be exciting work. Sometimes, it will be frustrating. But, it is always needed work. The question you will have to answer is this: "Is Christ worth it?"

There is no Christmas joy without commitment to Christ all year long. The price will be asked; will we be willing to pay it? One pastor told of a man in his church who seemed to be a wreck. He was somebody who couldn't complete a sentence when he tried to speak. His business was in shambles. His family problems were great. But he would always come to church faithfully. One day going to a funeral he rode with the preacher, and he told him this story. "I know you might find this hard to believe, but when I graduated from high school I was voted the most likely to succeed. I even won the oratory prize and gave the speech at our graduation exercises. People stopped me on the street to tell me that they were sure I would succeed whatever I did. I thought that God wanted me to serve him.

"Every time I went to church I got the feeling that he wanted to use my gifts in his ministry, but I resisted that call. I would always turn and walk away from it. You know the results of that. My life is a mess; my business is ruined; my family brings grief to me. I am telling you this because every time you have a chance to speak to young people about what to do with their lives, you can tell them that it will cost to say yes to Christ. But it will cost them more to say no to him."[3]

There is a price involved in following Christ, but I can tell you that I have seen those who have not followed him pay an even higher price in unhappiness and misery and emptiness. If we will make the commitment of our lives to Christ and are willing to pay the price he asks of us for service, then what we receive will be greater than anything we will ever have to pay.

Now what? Now that Christmas is over, what do we do? How can we catch it and keep it alive? We can do so by telling others the good news, by sharing what we have discovered. We can do so by trying each day to live what we say we believe. We can do so by making a commitment to Christ that is willing to pay whatever price is needed.

If we want to catch Christmas, the only way to do it is to let the Christ who came help us live for him each day. If we will do that, if we will make a serious effort to live and serve Christ each day, then Christmas and its spirit will stay with us. Try it and see if it is not so!

NOTES

1. Brian Harbour, "Possessions," *Proclaim* (Oct.-Dec. 1980), pp. 33-34.

2. Wilson Kilgore, "On Giving Up Too Soon," *Master Sermons*, Sept. 1981, p. 425.

3. John Claypool, "Hello and Goodbye," Sermon: Northminister Baptist Church, Jackson, Mississippi, 27 Jan. 1980, p. 8.

Series Three
The Sounds of Christmas

In order to help the Christmas story come alive, imagination is needed. One must try to put himself into the middle of the events and try to feel them, sense the importance of them, and hear them. I have tried to do that with this series, to imagine all of the sounds and noises that must have been part of the Christmas scene. These sounds then become the focal points to help understand the deeper meaning of the Christmas message.

Sermons

A Mother's Lullaby: A Noisy Inn
A Baby's Cry: A Soldier's Threat
An Angel's Song: And Laughter of Hope
A Prayer of Worship: A Shout of Praise

A MOTHER'S LULLABY

A Noisy Inn

(Luke 2:1-7)

I have begun to hear them already, the sounds of Christmas. They seem to be coming at me from everywhere. Already Christmas music is blaring at me from across the airways. Already television specials about Christmas have been on the screen. It seems that every day my children are reminding me of what they want for Christmas. And then there's that worst sound of all, the sound of the television and radio commercials telling me that unless I buy this or that I just cannot possibly have a very Merry Christmas.

The sounds are coming and I wish I could say that it was going to get better, but it isn't. The deeper we get into the Christmas season, the louder the sounds will come even to the point of getting on our nerves. I've already heard a couple of adults say, "Oh, no, it's not Christmas again. I just hope I can get through it."

That's a shame. It's a shame that Christmas has become for many a hectic, nerve-racking, tiring experience. But that's the way it is: so much to do, so many places to go, so much to buy, so many noises.

The danger of it all is that we will somehow miss what Christmas was meant to be. We will never really hear the noises and sounds that matter. That will be a shame, to go through the motions of celebrating Christmas, but never really doing it, never getting to the place where we once again fully understand what it means. I want us to try to hear some of the Christmas sounds because they can help us understand a lot about life then and about our lives now.

Let us consider these two sounds: a noisy inn and a mother's lullaby. We know the story of Mary and Joseph making their way to Bethlehem to enroll for the tax, coming there late at night, not finding a place in the inn because it was too full. Mary ends up in the back of the inn in a stable, and there she gave birth to Jesus. There were two sounds: The noisy inn, a symbol of the world's indifference and unconcern; a mother's lullaby, a symbol of the presence of God in the midst of this world. These sounds tell us something about now.

1. The sounds tell us that there is love in a world that too often doesn't seem to know it.

The inn was full. Why? Taxes! The Romans wanted everyone to enroll for taxes. It was a reminder to them that they were an oppressed people and had to pay for that. There was no love lost between the Romans and the Jewish people. I can imagine that in that inn there was a lot of bitter talk about the Romans. There was a knock on the door and a couple stood there. They needed a place, but there was no place. I wonder how many saw their plight? How many in that inn were going to have a baby? Did anyone feel concern enough to offer his room? No such offer was made. Instead, caught up in their own self-concerns, they did not notice the need before their doorstep—no room in the inn.

But then a baby was born in a stable, a place for animals. That stable was enough for God. A mother, I imagine, sang softly to her newborn baby. What an act of love that is. It's an act of love just to see a mother and a newborn baby. What a picture of love, but even more so here. The very Son of God was brought into the world to show the world how much God loved. While everyone was having a good time in the front of the noisy inn, in the back was the soft music of a mother's lullaby. Love in the world! Love had not been forgotten! Love was in the midst of a world that didn't know it and often didn't show it.

How contemporary that sounds. The noisy inn could be a symbol of our day. Often we are the indifferent and the uncaring. We are indifferent to the plight of the poor, the hungry, and the oppressed. Often we do not see them and do not want to see them. There is hatred that allows racism to grow. There is hatred in the words we sometimes speak of one another. Hatred is seen in crimes of violence that seem to have no concern for the victim. There are the many divorces where pain and suffering is the order of the day, child abuse and wife abuse, and so many other kinds of hurt. There is so little love, it seems, in the world in which we live.

It's easy to get to the place where we feel there is no love at all, but what Christmas tries to tell us is that behind the noisy inns, there is a mother's lullaby. There *are* people who care. There *are* people who love. Someone (was it the innkeeper?) did give Mary a place to stay and it was enough.

At Christmas, it's good to remember that there are people who are caring about the plight of the needy. Food is being sent to starving nations. Refugees are being taken in. People are standing up for the plight of the oppressed and the poor. There are black and white who are joining together in the fight for brotherhood believing, under God, that all people *are* brothers. It is good to remember that there are those who speak words of kindness and encouragement, that there are families who stay together in marriage for many years. There are children who grow up to be good citizens. There are people who would never think of being dishonest or crooked. There are good people in the world. There *is* love in the world in the midst of all the noises and sounds that are around us.

God hasn't left us. Love is real, even now. In a department store at Christmas, the clerks were wearing signs that said, "We care." However, at Christmas, it doesn't seem to be true. All the noises that were being heard in that department store were the noises of cash registers ringing up sales. There were angry people trying to elbow their way to get what they wanted. It was a hectic time, as it always is.

A boy came into that department store and he had a balloon filled with helium; it slipped out of his hand and stuck on the ceiling. The boy began to cry. A clerk saw it. She called downstairs to the janitor and said, "Get the ladder and climb up and get this balloon down for the little boy." He said, "Are you crazy?" After some persuasion, he brought his ladder up to the toy department and started climbing to get the balloon for the little boy.

All of a sudden, the cash registers were silent. People quit elbowing, trying to get positions at counters. Everybody was watching as that man climbed the ladder, reached out, got that balloon, and brought it back down to a boy whose face looked like a new sunrise. As that happened, everybody cheered. Then the ladder was taken away. The cash registers began to ring again. People began to try to get what they wanted again. Yet for just a moment, they had seen it. A tiny act of love in the midst of all the commotion of Christmas.[1]

There is still love here. There is still God here. We must look for it, see it, do it.

2. The sounds remind us that there is joy in a world that doesn't really have it.

There were a lot of people in that inn, all seeming to have a good time. I'm sure the laughter and the talk were loud but I'm also sure that there were a lot of people who were very unhappy. They had lots to be unhappy about. They were an oppressed people and couldn't fight back easily. They were unhappy because they had suffered much and it seemed like they would suffer even more. They were unhappy over the fact that they had sought a Messiah, believed one would come, but he never had and now they were beginning to believe he never would. In that noisy inn, there was probably a lot of drinking and loud noise, but it was all superficial, the shallow laughter trying to mask the despair and hopelessness.

Behind the loud noises of that inn, there was a mother's lullaby. Mary had her difficulties, too. She had to struggle with hardship. But she had a secret. She knew God had not left the world. She knew that God still loved her, that she was in his hands, and nothing could change that. She began to sing. It was a song of joy and love because she knew that God was there.

Our world is looking for a joy that's real and it tries everything to find it—games and parties, all kinds of sports, new cars, new houses, new husbands, new wives. People are trying to find joy but never find it. And Christmas is very frustrating for many because Christmas is supposed to be a time of great joy. But how do you find it when you don't have it? I think it's sad that so many celebrate the Christmas season by getting drunk, trying to cover up their emptiness. One woman who became an alcoholic traced the beginning of her plight to a Christmas party where, with her Christmas whiskey in her hand, she staggered to the bar and sang in discordant tones, "Silent Night, Holy Night."[2] Such superficial joy dies. It does not last. Suicide rises to great heights during the Christmas season. Depression overwhelms many during Christmas because they come face-to-face with the fact that they are not happy; they have not found joy.

The reason is simple. They have sought to find it in outside things and have not understood that joy begins from a relationship with God who made us all. Joy is found when he becomes part of our lives, and we remember that we are in his hands, and nothing can take him away from us. God has not left us. He has brought joy to the world.

One of the stories children like at Christmas is one called "The Grinch Who Stole Christmas." It is about a mean, evil Grinch who decided he didn't want the people in Whoville to enjoy Christmas. He took away everything that symbolized it. He stole all of the Christmas trees, all of the gifts, all the goodies that they made, all of the lights and tinsel. Everything that seemed to speak of Christmas, he stole. He said, "There, that will show them. Now they won't have Christmas." But the people of Whoville stood in the snow and joined hands and sang their Christmas songs of love and joy. They proved that the Grinch could steal everything about Christmas, but he couldn't steal Christmas, for Christmas was deep within their hearts.[3]

This is the secret we need to remember. Christmas is not what we do to celebrate it. Christmas is Christ dwelling within and if everything else is taken away there is still reason for joy. Christ is still with us.

3. The sounds of Christmas remind us that there is inner peace and confidence in the world that doesn't know where to get it.

Jesus was born into a world that lived on the edge of anxiety and fear. They lived with constant tension. They were uptight about the Romans, about taxes, about suffering, even about a God who seemed to have abandoned them. In that noisy inn were many who were not at ease inside. They had not found inner peace. But Mary had. For the song she sang was one of joy and one of confidence. She didn't complain about her situation. She didn't fuss about her accommodations. She didn't have any fears that God was gone; she knew better because of her experiences. Because of this birth, she knew that God was in this world and in control of it. He had not been defeated. He was not gone. He was there working out his purposes in the world, and she could trust him.

This is what Christmas tries to remind us. Christ is still Lord and Master of us all. We have not been left alone. We are not forgotten. God is still working out his purposes and always will; we can trust him to do that.

There was a little boy in a shopping mall who was sleeping in the midst of the noisy crowds. How could a little baby sleep in the midst of all of that noise? It was because the baby rested secure in the love of his mother's arms, confident that she would provide for his every need.

We ought to be the same in the midst of our own world. We ought to live in the confidence that our Father's love is secure. We ought to live in the confidence that when we are in his arms, that's the best place to be and he will not drop us. We ought to be living in faith and confidence that God can be trusted, that we can live in the midst of all the difficulties with a sense of peace inside that God is still God!

There was a man whose wife died. After they buried her, that night with his younger son he was trying to get to sleep. The boy was in the same bed with the father. It was dark in the room and the boy couldn't get to sleep. Finally, the boy said to the father, "Is your face turned toward me? If your face is turned toward me, I can go to sleep." The father said, "Yes, son. I'm looking right at you." After a while the boy went to sleep. The father, still distraught and still troubled, got out of his bed and went over to the window, looked up into the dark of night at all of the stars and said, "God, is your face turned toward me?"[4]

Christmas is the affirmation that God's face is always turned toward us and that is enough. There can be peace in our lives.

Here it comes, Christmas with all of its sounds and noises. What I hope you will do this Christmas is to try to hear in all of the noises the sounds of God speaking. Maybe you'll hear in a Christmas carol or in the "Merry Christmas" of a friend or in some moment of worship or even in a mother's lullaby, the voice of God telling you that love is real, that joy is possible, that peace is a reality.

The truth is that God has been trying to speak to us over and over and over; Christmas is one loud word of God to us hoping that maybe we will hear for the first time, if we've never heard before, that God is real, that God does care. If we will trust him, then we will know life like never before. Listen this Christmas for the sounds of God as he tries, once again, to speak to you.

NOTES

1. Stan Jones, "We Care," *Faith at Work,* Dec. 1978, p. 11.

2. Richard R. Potter, "If My Brother Stumbles," *Survey,* Dec. 1968, p. 15.

3. Jo Carr, *Advent* (Nashville: Abingdon, 1976), p. 27.

4. Ray F. Chester, "On Suffering as a Christian," *Master Sermons,* Mar. 1977, pp. 123-124.

A BABY'S CRY

A Soldier's Threat

(Matt. 2:13-18)

There are those who say that it's very hard to get into the spirit of Christmas, what with all of the problems we're facing in the world. So instead of blinking lights and bright tinsel, maybe there ought to be darkness.

We can understand that this Christmas; many of the sounds that we hear are unpleasant ones. There are the sounds of angry mobs as they demonstrate against the United States around our world. There are the sounds of gunfire as terrorists attack a bus and kill. We realize that there is no peace in our world. There are sounds of a crying mother as she watches helplessly as her child dies because he doesn't have enough to eat in the land of Cambodia. Then there are the sounds of tears falling from those who are sick and struggle with pain, those who stand by the lonely graves, children of broken homes who search for love, and the lonely who seem to find no friends.

These are difficult times and we do have difficult problems to face. It does seem like it is very hard to sing "Joy to the World" in times like these. But what we need to understand is that Christmas was not born into a world that was antiseptic and clean and free from problems. That first Christmas was born into a world full of problems and heartaches. There were those in that day who didn't feel like singing songs of joy. It was for such a time that Christmas came, and it is for such a time as this that Christmas has come. Let us listen to some of the unpleasant sounds of that first Christmas but yet try to understand the word they speak to our day.

Let us hear a soldier's threat and a baby's cry. The birth of Christ was not welcomed by everyone. Herod, the king, didn't want it. He was afraid of anyone that might grow up and become a threat to his rulership, so he sought to discover where the baby was. When he couldn't do that, he had every boy two years old or under in the area killed. Soldiers and their threats as they walked up to the door, the heart wrenching cry of the babies as they died—a horrible thought, but it is there in the midst of our Christmas story. What could that say to us?

1. There is suffering in the world but also a God who comes to share it.

The Bible is always realistic. It looks at life as it really is and the first Christmas story is no exception. Christmas happened in a world full of suffering and pain. There was the suffering of the people who were oppressed. They couldn't go where they wanted to go, couldn't do what they wanted to do. They were the conquered and they suffered accordingly. There was the suffering of the people in poverty and people struggling with sickness. The living conditions in that day were not good and many had to struggle just to make it through the day. There was the suffering that Herod caused. Did the parents understand why little babies were killed? I'm sure they didn't. It was horrible, such innocent suffering!

But Jesus had to face danger, too. Mary and Joseph had to flee by night in order to keep him from being found by Herod's soldiers. I imagine that you could have heard the sound of that baby crying because he was awakened in the middle of the night, crying from the travel, from the bumps in the road, and from the lack of sleep. He didn't know in his tiny body what was going on. It was just unpleasant and hard to take.

Yet that baby was a reminder of hope. That baby was God who had come into the world in the midst of all of its suffering. That baby was to grow up to face all the suffering, endure it and struggle with it all. God came in Christ to let us know that he understood our suffering. He faced it himself—loneliness, despair, rejection, physical pain, inner pain. He came to help his people not to run away from their troubles, not to run around their troubles, but to go through them.

This is what Christmas tries to remind us. It reminds us that there is a God who understands our struggles and our pain. He has come to share it with us. In our suffering we're not alone. Elie Wiesel, a very famous Jewish writer who lived through Auschwitz, told of an experience in his book, *Night,* of a young adolescent boy prisoner who was being executed. He wrote, "One day when we came back from work, we saw three gallows rearing up in the assembly place . . . Roll call . . . S. S. all around us, machine guns trained . . . three victims in chains—one of them a sad eyed youth." The S. S. seemed more preoccupied, more disturbed than usual. To hang a young boy in front of thousands of spectators was no light matter.

Three victims mounted together onto the chairs. The three necks were placed within the nooses. "Long live liberty," cried the two adults. But the child was silent.

"Where is God? Where is he?" someone behind me asked. At the sign from the head of the camp the three chairs tipped over. Total silence throughout the camp. On the horizon, the sun was setting.

"Bare your heads," yelled the head of the camp. His voice was raucous. We were weeping.

Then the march past began. The two adults were dead. Their tongues were swollen. But the third rope was still moving; being so light, the child was still alive. For more than half an hour he stayed there, struggling between life and death, and we had to look him full in the face. Behind me I heard the same man ask, "Where is God now? Where is he?" I replied, "Here he is—he is hanging here on the gallows."[1]

While it may be hard to understand, this is the truth of the Cross, in the midst of our suffering is God. He suffers with us. He has come to tell us that we do not have to fear the darkness for the darkness will not overwhelm us because he is within it.

Dietrich Ritschl told of an experience when they bombed a city in Germany in 1944. In that bombing, thousands of people were killed. After the bombing had passed, he was lying in the railroad station looking up at the fires burning all over the city. He caught a glimpse of an inscription on the top of that railroad station. It said, "Beyond the stars, there must live a gracious Father." He said, "I do not want such a God."[2]

Neither do I. I don't want a God who dwells beyond the stars. I want a God who dwells with me, who understands what it is to face what I face, who understands my pain and my suffering. What Christmas reveals is that this is the kind of God we have, one who comes into the midst of our suffering to help us share it, face it, and conquer it.

2. There is uncertainty in the world but also a God who helps us face it.

Mystery and uncertainty certainly surrounded the early Christmas story. Mary and Joseph did not have time to enjoy the birth of their baby.

Instead, they had to snatch him up and run. The baby must have cried as they made their way down to Egypt. What was going to happen to them? They didn't know. Egypt was a strange place to them. How would they survive? How would they live? What would they do? Would the soldiers follow and find them? I'm sure that with each knock on the door, their hearts must have been full of fear and anxiety.

Also, what would God do with them? They had heard that this One was going to grow up to be the Savior of the world. How would God work that and what would God require of them? They did not know. They lived on the edge of mystery and uncertainty, but they lived with God and that made the difference. For God had already gone before them to prepare for the birth. They had seen that. Therefore, they lived with the belief that God would go before them to prepare the way. Before them lay the unknown, but before them also lay God, and he was enough. They believed that whatever they would face, he would be there and would be able to handle it.

We need to hear that because we live today in the midst of great uncertainty. We do not know what is going to happen. Will we have to go to war? Will inflation get worse? Will I have enough money to retire on? Is the pain I feel serious? Will I ever get married? Will I ever get a job? Will I ever graduate? On the questions go and we have no answers. We do not know. Tomorrow is a mystery and will always be.

However, Christmas tries to help us remember what we do know and that is this: God is in the tomorrow of our lives. While we do not know what will come, he does and he will help us face it. It is an axiom of our faith that God will never ask us to do anything that we cannot do, but it is also true that God will never ask from us anything he will not help us to do. This is the faith we live by; in the midst of all the uncertainty and mystery God is there and it will be all right.

A little boy went to bed and his father turned off the light. The boy didn't like that. He didn't like the dark, but the father said, "There's nothing to be afraid of. It will be all right. Go on to sleep." But that didn't work. The little boy would cry a little, afraid of the dark. Finally, his father went in and put up the shade of the window. There was a full moon and the light of the moon shown in the room. The little boy said, "Is that God's light?" "Yes, that's God's light. That's the moon." The boy said, "Does God ever turn off his light?" The father answered very carefully, "No son, God never goes to sleep. He never turns off his light."

The boy said, "Well, if God never turns off his light, then there's no reason for me to be afraid is there?" Off to sleep he went.[3]

The darkness frightens us. We want some light. Christmas tells us light has come. God never slumbers nor sleeps. He is there before us, preparing the way for us, and we can go forward knowing he will go with us.

3. There is death in the world, but also a God who overcomes it.

How horrible it must have been to see the soldiers with their swords, to hear the cries of the babies as they died. But there is the paradox of Christmas. There is birth, and there is death. One baby is born; many babies die. That event brings us face-to-face with the fact of death and its horribleness. The strange fact of the Christmas story is that this very baby who had to run for his life was the One who grew up to conquer death. He grew up to face it. He climbed the cross and suffered a terrible death, but he overcame it. He rose from the dead. This child had come to make sure that death was no longer to be feared. He would conquer death. Those who put their faith in him would discover that he is with them forever.

God will stay with us always. We need to hear that again. As a pastor, I have stood by many gravesides. Death has brought tears to many in our church fellowship. Death is a part of our lives and we cannot overlook it, but Christmas sounded the death knell for death. Christmas reminds us that God has conquered death. Life with him is forever. Death is not the end but a passageway to that which is greater and better and more. Do we remember that?

There was a family whose four-year-old boy had died of leukemia. On that first Christmas afterwards, it was very difficult for the family. The mother wrote, "We were handling it all right, trying to get by." The time came to decorate the Christmas tree, and that was a little bit too much for her, and she began to cry. The oldest boy named Jim, who was six years old, said, "You're missing Dougie, aren't you?" "Yes, I'm missing him." The little boy said, "I miss Dougie too, but isn't Christmas the celebration of Christ's birthday?" "Yes." "Isn't Dougie with Christ?" "Yes." Then Jim said, "I just suppose that he's having more fun than we are right now, don't you think?"[4]

From the mouths of little children came words of faith. Those who have put their faith in the hands of God are always in the hands of God and nothing in the world or beyond can ever, ever change it.

This Christmas, there will be horrible sounds to hear. It was the same with the world into which Christ was born. Suffering, uncertainty, and death—it was all there. Christ faced it all, but it was to such a world and for such a world that he came to help us struggle with these enemies and defeat them.

Wes Seeliger, a Methodist minister, told of one of his family events at Christmas. They were making a Christmas manger scene and everybody was contributing putting in the animals and the statues of Mary and Joseph and the little baby. His five-year-old boy, Scott, suddenly ran back into his room and brought out a *Tyrannosaurus rex* to put in the manger. That's a big dinosaur. He placed it overlooking Mary and Joseph and the baby. He looked so menacing, so terrifying in that manger.

Seeliger said, "I was tempted to try to tell Scott, 'Look, that dinosaur is out of date. He lived millions of years before Christ was born. He wasn't around during Christ's time.'" He also was tempted to tell him that it didn't look good in the manger; it wasn't good for the decorative qualities of it all. Then he said, "I caught myself because I realized that, in essence, he had caught a truth of Christmas. For Christmas came to help us face the dinosaurs life places before us—those menacing terrors that seem to be so strong, so powerful. Christmas came to defeat them."[5]

Since Christmas came, we do not need to fear ultimately the dinosaur of suffering because Christ will help us overcome it; or the dinosaur of uncertainty, for Christ will be there to walk with us; or the dinosaur of death, for Christ will help us overcome it. This is the word the world and we need to hear more than any other: whatever happens to us, whatever happens to this world or in this world, it will not be anything that can destroy God or what God has done. What God has done in Christ is forever. Therefore, despair can be swallowed up in hope; death can be swallowed up in life; and Christmas can be celebrated with joy and love because God has come, is come, and always will be here for us all.

NOTES

1. Richard L. Gronhovd, "It's Christmas and Where is God?," *Faith at Work*, Dec. 1979, p. 15.

2. Eugene E. Laubach, "The Baby and the Mad King," Sermon: Riverside Church, New York, New York, 1 Jan. 1978, p. 2.

3. Clarence Forsberg, "A Golden Text for the Seventies," *Pulpit Preaching,* Dec. 1969, pp. 17-18.

4. Jo Carr, *Advent* (Nashville: Abingdon, 1977), pp. 50-51.

5. James Flamming, "Preaching Resources for Special Occasions," *Proclaim* (Oct.-Dec.), 1976, p. 39.

AN ANGEL'S SONG

And Laughter of Hope

(Luke 2:8-20)

She is a housewife and the mother of four children. She doesn't have many of the frills of life, doesn't have much time for herself. She works from sunup to sundown trying to survive and she's not famous at all. In fact, according to society's standards, she's not very important. But there she is, working hard, day by endless day. Does Christmas have a word for her?

There he is, working in a factory that makes parts for railroad cars. Six days a week he works, from early morning till late in the afternoons, standing in front of a machine pushing this button and turning this crank. The pay isn't all that good. He has a wife and three children to support. He hasn't much education because he had to drop out in order to get a job to survive. This is his life and probably his future, destined to spend years standing in front of that machine pushing this button and turning that crank. Does Christmas have a word for him?

They go where the work is, those migrants. If you need fruit to be picked, they will pick it. They pack up their families and travel long distances to find work. The living conditions aren't the best. Pay is barely adequate, if adequate at all. They live lives of quiet desperation hoping to make it through another day, another month, or another year. This is the way life is for them, and they fear it is the way it will always be. Does Christmas have a word for them?

It's an important question. There are so many people like them, strugglers trying to survive. People who will never be rich or famous, who'll never be able to travel around the world, who will never have enough money to visit the Riviera or even Virginia Beach. They are the strugglers; and many of them are like us, trying hard just to get by. If Christmas doesn't have a word for them, does it really have a word for us?

Christmas does have a word for them. That is what these sounds tell us: an angel's song and laughter that is born of hope. Isn't it significant that the announcement of the birth of Christ came to shepherds, hard workers, those that society needed but didn't consider important. They were next to the last on the scale of occupational work, just above the tanners.

They were the insignificant, but to them—not to the king, not to those in power, not to those rich or famous—the angel came. How it must have brought them hope. How it must have brought laughter to their lives to know that God came to them and through them to all. What was the Christmas word given to the strugglers of the world? What is that Christmas word to us?

1. We matter; each of us is loved.

God came to the world in a baby to show that he is love. The announcement of this birth came to those who were considered unlovely shepherds, lonely people who carried out their difficult work in relative obscurity. I'm sure they wondered, did anybody really notice them? Did anybody care about them? Who worried over them? For the most part, it seemed they had no one. But the angel came to them and tried to let them know that God cared, that God noticed, that God worried over them, that they mattered to him. "I bring you good tidings of great joy. Unto you is born, a Savior, Christ the Lord" (vv. 10-11, AT).

Shepherds were given this word and they were overwhelmed with it. Just think of it! God came to *them*! The angel told *them*! They were noticed, they were cared about, they did matter. The God who made all that is came down to earth and they were the ones to hear about it. How their value went up to know that they were loved by God.

There are many I have met who wonder if they matter. A little boy in the orphans' home watched as the soldiers brought gifts at Christmas. One soldier stood before the little boy and asked, "What do you want for Christmas?" The boy simply said, "Sir, I just want to be loved."

There are many who want just that. A teenager robs a store, and the clues he leaves are easy to follow. He is caught, and what he is saying by his negative action is, "Please, won't somebody notice me? I want to be loved." A housewife slaves for many years and then one day she just walks out. She leaves home to get a job, go to school, or find another home. By these actions she says in a sense, "I want to be noticed. I want to feel that I am loved." A man lies drunk in some alley in some godforsaken skid row. Life has been cruel to him, too hard for him. He feels lonely and forsaken as he lies beside his bottle. But he is crying out, "Please, I just want to be loved."

Do you ever wonder if anybody notices you? Do you matter to anyone? Does anybody care about you? Listen to the angel's song: Unto *you* is born this day a Savior. Unto YOU! For God loved you so much that he came down to this earth in the form of Christ to ultimately climb a cross to die for your sins. That's how much *you* matter to God. The angel's song is an announcement that you are known by God, noticed by God; you matter to God. While no one else may see or hear or care for you, the God who made it all does notice and does care.

D. T. Niles, a missionary to India, met a shepherd boy tending sheep. He asked the boy, "How many sheep do you have?" The boy said, "I don't know, I can't count." "Well, how do you know if you lose any, since you can't count?" The boy said, "I can't count, but every sheep I have has a name and if they are missing, I may not know how many are missing, but I know which sheep are because I know each sheep by name."[1]

In a sense, God treats us the same way. We're not numbers to God. We are names and hurts and hopes and desires. The orphan boy who said he wanted to be loved found love in the heart of a soldier who reached out and made the boy a home. Likewise, God has come down to answer our cry for love, to tell us we are loved. He reaches out to offer us a home. What a difference it would make in our lives if we lived with the certainty day by day that each of us were loved!

2. The angel's song: life has meaning because God is in it.

I'm sure these shepherds wondered a lot about life. They had a lot of time to sit around the fire and meditate. I'm sure they wondered what they were here for, what was the purpose of their lives. Were their lives headed anywhere? What was going to happen in the end? I'm sure they wondered if there was a God. They had been waiting for a Messiah for hundreds of years, but no Messiah had come. Maybe they wondered if God would ever come. I'm sure they wondered if life made sense because there was much in it that seemed to be senseless—suffering and oppression and boredom.

Suddenly, the angel came and sang a song that God had come into life itself. What a difference that made! Not only did these shepherds learn that they mattered, they also learned that life mattered. It was God's life and God cared about it. God was in it working out his purposes. There was much they didn't understand, but this they did. Life was sacred because it was God's and, because it was, life was not just headed nowhere. Life was headed somewhere, and everything they did was important if offered to God. Even such a task that seemed unimportant to the eyes of the world, like tending sheep, could be used by God to work out his purposes. God was no longer distant, God was immersed in the middle of life trying to bring out of it what he wanted. Purpose had come to the world.

A woman was interviewed on television. She worked at a tire and rubber company making parts for airplanes. She described her work. She was at a big table with a big piece of rubber material. "Where did that material come from?" she was asked. "I don't know. It's just there from the warehouse." "What do you do?" She said, "I take a little pattern, put it on this piece of material and cut around it." "What is that design used for?" She said, "I haven't the faintest idea." "What do you do with it after you cut it out?" "I give it to the girl next to me on the line." "What does she do with it?" "She punches holes in it." "What is that for?" "I haven't the faintest idea."[2]

Here was her life: sitting at a table, cutting out patterns in rubber. She didn't know what for, she really didn't know why. She just did it and that was her existence. There are many who live like that, who just go through the motions of life and never understand what it is all for. What's the meaning of it? Where is the sense of it? No rhyme or reason to life. You just get up and do your work and go to bed and get up and do your work and go to bed. They never put it all together, never see any purpose moving through it all. Does this sound like you?

A minister got an anonymous letter from a teenager. It said, "I'm from a broken home, an unhappy home, and please, in some sermon you preach on Sunday, could you give some inspiring words to someone who hasn't found any meaning in life?"[3] What inspiring words would you speak? How would you try to tell them that there is meaning? Here are the only inspiring words I know: God loves you; God has come for you; God is in the world trying to reach you, trying to help you, trying to guide you through life.

Life is not insane. It has meaning and purpose. If we unite ourselves with him, we will find the hope of it. We will be able to laugh a little bit more because we will see that whatever we do, if done in service to Christ, is worthwhile. It will not be in vain. That is what the angels said. We matter. What we do matters.[4]

3. The angel's song said that faith matters, it is not in vain.

The shepherds were Jewish folk with a rich religious heritage. They had worshiped. They carried out the sacrifices and rituals. I'm sure that they longed for the coming of the Messiah. They were God's chosen people, but they were oppressed. They were God's chosen people, but they were suffering. They were God's chosen people, but their faith didn't seem to do them any good. What good was it to believe and have to go through all that they did?

The angel's song came to tell them that their faith was right, that the values they were living by—honesty and integrity and justice and righteousness and love—were the right values. They were the values that one day would triumph. They were the values that would bring them life, abundant and eternal. The shepherds had their faith affirmed in the song of the angel.

Doubts had entered, faith had waivered, but now it was sustained and encouraged. They could go out worshiping, praising, glorifying God because they knew that the way they walked was the right way; the values they lived by were the right values; the God they worshiped would be the God who triumphed. With more faith and more hope they went back to those hills to tend those sheep, confident that the little faith that they were able to muster mattered.

There are those days when I wonder: Is it really worth it to live this Christian faith? Is it really worth it to live the values of this faith and not the values that the world shows us? Have you ever wondered that? Why should we try to live by love when so many people live with hate and seem to get along better? Why should we live with honesty and integrity when so many cheat and seem to make a go of it? Why should we live by purity and morality when those who throw moral standards out the door seem to survive? Why should we keep our faith? Why do we need to worship and pray and study the Bible when there are so many who don't, and they seem to get along all right?

Christmas tells us why. Because these are the values that will last. These are the values that will triumph in the end because they are the values of Christ. He is the only one who will sit on the throne of life at the end. While there is difficulty, darkness, and hardship in the middle of life, Christ is there working out his purposes. We can live with the hope that we will conquer, that the values we believe in will be the values that triumph.

Some years ago there was a professor who taught history in a college. He moved up to administrative assistant, but suddenly, he got the word that his job was being phased out. His future looked bleak. It looked as if he would have to move out of the house that he lived in with his wife and two children. He didn't know where he would find any work. The doubt and the despair of it overwhelmed him and he began to do something he'd forgotten how to do for a long time: he began to pray again. In desperation he prayed, trying to find some hope, some answer.

In one of his prayers, he recorded this vision. He was standing on a cliff, and he felt good. The cliff overlooked the sea, the warmth of the sun was beating on his back, and the smell of the salt water was in his nose. The sea gulls were screeching overhead. He had a very warm feeling about that moment. He looked down in the water and saw a bottle. He could see that that bottle had a note in it. He rushed down to the beach to retrieve that bottle because he was sure that it was God's word for him. He eagerly tore the note out. This was his word. The note was in Latin. "Hodie Christus Natus Est." "Today Christ is born." He thought how disappointing, in the midst of all of his problems and difficulties, those words, "Today Christ is born." He thought about it and began to realize what it meant: in the middle of his life Christ was born, not dead. Since he was not dead, there was hope, there was a tomorrow. The man did not have to be overcome by despair and hopelessness. There was more.[4]

This is what Christmas tries to tell us. "Today Christ is born." He still is and always will be. In all that we have to deal with, we have that truth walking alongside of us. Christ is born, and our faith is not in vain.

So hear the angel's song, a song that told the shepherds that they mattered, that what they did mattered, that faith mattered. That was God's word to those strugglers and it is God's word for all the strugglers in our world today. It is God's word to us. We matter to God. What we do matters to God. Our faith matters. God is with us; we can listen to the angel's song with new hope.

> Hark! the herald angels sing,
> "Glory to the newborn King;
> Peace on earth, and mercy mild;

God and sinners reconciled."
Joyful, all ye nations, rise,
Join the triumph of the skies;
With angelic hosts proclaim,
"Christ is born in Bethlehem!"[5]

Christ has been born. He has come for you and for me. Therefore, for us there is always laughter, laughter born of hope because Christ is born forever.

NOTES

1. Arthur Fay Sueltz, *Deeper into John's Gospel* (New York: Harper and Row, 1979), p. 94.

2. *Pulpit Resource*, (Oct.-Dec. 1978), p. 19.

3. David A. Maclennan, "Priming the Preacher's Pump," *Clergy Journal*, Apr. 1978, p. 11.

4. John Killinger, "Priorities in Preaching" in *Priorities*, Proceedings of the Christian Life Commission, Southern Baptist Convention, Jackson, Mississippi, Mar. 21-23 1977, p. 54.

5. Charles Wesley, "Hark! The Herald Angels Sing," *Baptist Hymnal* (Nashville: Convention Press, 1975), p. 83.

A PRAYER OF WORSHIP

A Shout of Praise

(Matt. 2:7-12; Luke 2:20)

You try to select a gift carefully because you want it to be just right. It's a special gift for a special person. You find it and wrap it nicely and, when the time comes, you give it to her. You wait with eager anticipation to see how she will receive your gift. She takes it and tears off the paper and opens the box. What happens? What response will she make?

You could feel disappointment because on her face could be written disgust. She doesn't like your gift. It's not what she wanted. It doesn't bring her the joy that you thought it would. Your gift is rejected and you feel that you are, too. It makes you feel sick inside.

Or her face could light up when she sees what you have given her. It is what she wanted. It is what she needed. It makes her so happy. She wants your gift. She receives it and receives you. What a warm feeling you have inside.

At Christmas, it matters how we give—hopefully, from love. But it also matters how we receive—hopefully, joyfully and gratefully. Giving and receiving is what Christmas is all about. Christmas is the time when God, in love, gave us the gift of his Son and the celebration of Christmas occurs when we receive his Son joyfully and gratefully. The most important questions for us to answer this Christmas are these: How have we responded to the coming of Christ? Have we received him or rejected him? Have we ignored him or followed him? What have we done with the gift God gave?

That gift was salvation—God trying to make a way for us to once again be back together with him. It was like that in the beginning of time, God and man walking together as one. Then Adam and Eve decided they didn't like it that way. They didn't want to live like God. Adam and Eve wanted to live their own way, so they rebelled against God and brought into the world misery and heartache and pain and all

115

that went with it. When they realized what they'd done they tried to undo it, but they couldn't. Nothing they did would overcome the consequences of their sin and rebellion against God. So at Christmas, God decided to do something about it once and for all. He came himself to undo the consequences of all our sin. God made it possible for him and us to be reconciled once more.

God came and the big question was, "Would he be received?" Unless that happened, he could accomplish nothing. Hear the sounds of Christmas in our story. There's a sound of a prayer, prayer of worship being uttered by Wise Men who had been looking for him for some time. They found him and fell on their knees and worshiped him. Then, if you listen, you can hear the shouts of praise coming forth from the mouths of the shepherds. They went to see the baby and when they saw him they went out "glorifying and praising God" (v. 20). He had come! Will Christmas become real for us? Will we receive God's gift at Christmas? If we do, what will it mean for us?

1. It is a gift of forgiveness for our past sins.

Why all the prayers, why all the praise over a baby boy? Because of what he meant to their lives: forgiveness for their sins. They needed it. They had lived on the other side of God far too long, and it wasn't pleasant. There was too much suffering involved with it. There was suffering under the oppression of the Romans. Once Israel had been a great nation, but they wouldn't listen to God. They disobeyed him and now they were weak. Instead of being the rulers they were the ruled.

There was the suffering that always comes when God's laws are disobeyed. There was a lack of love between people. Justice was seldom found in the land. They showed no mercy to one another. Guilt dwelt inside of them. Something was wrong with them. They went to the Temple and worshiped and went through the rituals prescribed for their sins, but they left the Temple with the guilt still inside.

That was why God came. He came at Christmas to tell them that he loved them and would not give up on them. He would give them a new chance at life. He would begin with their sins. We know that the baby grew up to eventually climb a cross and die for their sins. He paid the penalty for them. He died the death that sin should have brought them. Through all of this, God was saying that the rebellion was past history. It didn't matter any more. All that mattered was what they did today and from now on. The prayer of worship and the shout of praise came from the realization that their past sins were gone, and they had before them a new chance to obey God.

I read of a recipe book that had been recalled. You hear of cars being recalled but I never heard of a cookbook being recalled. This one was. It was recalled because they made a mistake in one of the recipes. In making a particular dish the way the recipe said to make it, they had neglected one of the basic elements of water. If you made it just as the recipe said, it would blow up in your face. They recalled the book to prevent that.[1]

How true this is about life. If we try to live by the wrong directions, if we try to follow our directions and not God's, it is guaranteed that someplace, sometime, somewhere, we're going to have an explosion on our hands. Life will fall in on us. We will discover that sin is too strong. It has more power than we thought. There are signs in our world today that sin has taken hold of us and that explosions have occurred. Suicide is always higher during the Christmas season than any other time of the year, but all during the year suicides have been rising. One out of two couples that get married end it in divorce. They do not know how to love one another. Did you know that two years ago, 20 percent of the babies born in Norfolk, Virginia, were illegitimate, including one to a ten-year-old girl? We have often had wrong concepts of love. Alcoholics and drug addicts number in the millions, those who can't cope with life and seek to escape from it. The psychiatry business is booming beyond imagination as millions go week by week to try to discover why they are no longer happy.

Can you identify with them? Do you know what I'm talking about? Do you know anything of the pain and the misery and the unhappiness of it all? If so, you know what it means to suffer the consequences of sin. We are all sinners, but what can we do about it? Ignore our sin? No, because it won't go away. Work harder and try to get busy? No, because sin stays. The longer we don't deal with it, the deeper the pain gets.

At Christmas, God tells us what to do with it. Give it to him. That's what he came for, to tell us that on our own we cannot overcome sin. He will! What we need to do is to let our sins go and to receive his gift of forgiveness. When we give our sins to God, we can forget them and go on.

There was a preteen who was in a tragic accident in which he was charged with involuntary manslaughter. The guilt of it haunted him all of his days. He wanted somebody to punish him because he thought he was evil. He stole a car one night and got caught by the police. He poured out this story to the probation officer of how he should be punished for what he did. The probation officer said just one statement. "Son, just because you made a mistake doesn't mean *you* were a mistake."[2]

We need to hear that again. God knew what he was doing when he made us. We have all made mistakes, but these mistakes can be forgiven. God does give us a new chance if only we will receive this gift he's brought.

2. There is the gift of help for present troubles.

They had them, these shepherds. They struggled with all of the problems that we do: suffering and sickness, frustration and despair, loneliness, doubt, and death. They wondered how they could make it through the day, how they could make it through the night. Christmas came to tell them how. God would help them. The God who came in Christ experienced and faced everything that they faced. He understands all of our problems.

There was help for their problems. For their suffering and sickness, there was healing or the strength to deal with it. For their despair and frustration, there was courage to go another step. For their loneliness, there was a sense of his presence. For doubt, there was a strengthening of faith; for death, a reminder that it could be overcome. Christ came to deliver them from their moment of trouble.

We need to hear that. We are no different. We struggle with these problems. Suffering and sickness hit us. Depression and frustration come often. Loneliness—have you ever felt that? Doubt—how many times have you wondered even about God? Death—far too many times, we stand in the presence of that. How can we go on?

Christmas tells us how. With his help God moves in mysterious ways in our lives. He deals with all of us differently, but his grace does move. For some, he may speak through a friend. For others, it may be a sense of peace that overwhelms you. For others, it may be courage that you strangely find to stand up and go forward. For some, God may speak through worship or music. God speaks in his way. He works in his way. We need to be open to live our lives with the realization that God is in it, and we must be open to receive the help that God gives us.

Let me share with you a story I heard from a man in Indiana. He and his family received something unexpected last Christmas: their home burned on Christmas Eve. It was a large, old house they had remodeled themselves. The fire started in some defective wiring. They lost everything except a few picture albums, a small table that had belonged to the man's grandmother, and a few clothes they managed to throw out a window. They spent Christmas Eve in a neighbor's house, shocked and grieved by what had happened. On Christmas Day, they walked through the snow to inspect the charred ruins of the home. They were grateful, the man said, that none of them had been hurt.

That afternoon, they began to receive visits and phone calls from people all over the city. Most people who came brought presents: clothes, food, toys for the children, poinsettias, and other things. Two builders who were out of work came and offered their services free to help rebuild the house. "When we went to bed on Christmas Eve," the man said, "we were exhausted and sick at heart. We thought it was the worst Christmas we had ever seen. But by the time it was over, we realized it was probably the best we'd ever had because we learned what wonderful folks our friends and neighbors are." "Would you do it over again?" I asked. "Not by choice," he said. "But looking back on it, it was a warm and beautiful experience."[3]

That is a tremendous message. God comes through others so unexpectedly. Christmas means that, in the midst of all of our struggles, there is God. With God there is always the possibility of joy, of love and life, if we would receive it.

3. There is the gift of hope for future steps.

They clung to hope. The shepherds waited desperately for a Messiah to come and help them. The Wise Men scanned the skies for who knows how long looking for some sign that God was there. That's all it seemed they had to cling to, especially those shepherds. They had no wealth, no prestige, no power. All they had was hope that God would not forget them, that God was still in control of the world. That's all they had.

Christmas told them that it was enough. Hope was born again in Bethlehem. Their hope was not in vain. God had not forgotten. God would help. God was in control of the world and they could pray a prayer of worship and shout a song of praise because they could go back to all of their difficult tomorrows with the assurance that the hope they lived by was true.

We live by hope, too. Sometimes in our world, it seems the only thing we have left is hope. It seemed to me this Christmas that a lot of the Christmas trees were put up early this year, the lights went on earlier than I can remember in past Christmases. My feeling is that many people did it because they were desperately looking for some hope in the midst of the dark times we live in. Maybe bringing on the lights at Christmas reminds them of times of love and joy. Maybe if they turned on the lights, the darkness wouldn't seem so dark.

Christmas tells us that a light has come into the world that can never go out, and the light is God. He has come to dwell with us and will always dwell with us. He has come to remind us that the hope we have is not in humanity; our ultimate hope is in God and what he can do. What we know about God is that nothing—war, inflation, suffering, tragedy, death—nothing in the world can stop God from being God. Therefore, those of us who have put our hope in him can go forward to face whatever comes.

There was a painting in the fifteenth century done by Robert Campin. In one of the frames, the angels announced to Mary that she was going to be the mother of the Christ child. Then in another panel, there was a picture of Joseph sitting at his carpenter bench; of all things, he was making mousetraps. How odd it seemed. Here was the announcement that God was going to come into the world and there was Joseph, who was going to play a major part in it, sitting at a bench making mousetraps. Does that make sense? Sure it does, for it tells us that Joseph was carrying on with great confidence in God. Life was going on and there was no reason to give up hope. There was no reason to panic. He could sit there at his carpenter's bench and make his mousetraps because he knew God was in the world and over it.[4]

We can go our own ways, making our mousetraps, keeping our houses, steering our ships, teaching in our schools, doing all the things that we do, not panicking but living with the confidence that God is and always will be. We're in his hands. Our hope will not fail us ever.

These are the gifts that God has brought us at Christmas. I can imagine again that this Christmas, as in all others, God waits eagerly to see what we will do with his gifts. Here's forgiveness. Will we take it? Here is help for present troubles. Will we use it? Here is hope for future steps. Will we live by it?

The only way we can do that is to let Christ live in us. The tragedy of

Christmas is that we can celebrate all its events but never take time to welcome into our lives its Christ. In Italy, Saint Nicholas doesn't bring the gifts to the children on Christmas morning. It's someone named Befana. There's a legend about her written in poetry:

> Befana, the housewife, scrubbing her pane,
> Saw three old sages ride down the lane.
> Saw three gray travelers pass her door—
> Gaspar, Balthazar and Melchior.
>
> "Where journey you, sirs?" she asked of them.
> And Gaspar answered, "To Bethlehem,
> For we have news of a marvelous thing;
> Born in a stable is Christ the King."
>
> "Give Him my welcome!" Balthazar smiled,
> "Come with us, mistress, to greet the child."
> "Oh, happily, happily would I fare
> Were my dusting through and I'd polished the stair."
> Old Melchior leaned on his saddle horn,
> "Then send but a gift to the small newborn."
>
> "Oh, gladly, gladly, I'd send Him one
> Were my cupboards clean and my weaving done.
> I'd give Him a robe to warm His sleep.
> But first I must mend the fire and sweep.
> As soon as ever I've baked my bread,
> I'll fetch Him a pillow for His head.
> And a coverlet, too." Befana said.
> "When the rooms are aired and the linen dry,
> I'll look to the Babe." But the three rode by.
> She worked for a day and a night and a day,
> Then, gifts in her hands, took up her way.
> But she never could find where the Christ child lay.
>
> And still she wanders at Christmastide,
> Houseless, whose house was all her pride,
> Whose heart was tardy, whose gifts were late;

Wanders and knocks at every gate,

Crying, "Good people, the bells begin!

Put off your toiling and let love in."[5]

God pleads with us to let him in, for only then can it ever be Christmas.

NOTES

1. Thomas D. Lea, "A Missing Ingredient," *Proclaim*, (Oct.-Dec.), 1979, p. 29.

2. Arthur Fay Sueltz, *Deeper into John's Gospel* (New York: Harper and Row, 1979), p. 14.

3. John Killinger, "What Are You Expecting for Christmas?" Sermon: First Presbyterian Church, Lynchburg, Virginia, 6 Dec. 1981, p. 6.

4. Roland P. Perdue, "Well, Somebody's Got to Make the Mousetraps!", *Master Sermons*, Dec. 1979, p. 614.

5. Jo Carr, *Advent* (Nashville: Abingdon, 1976), pp. 40-41.

Appendix

There are other ideas that can be used to preach Christmas as a series. Here are several other series that I have done.

Christmas Symbols: Insight into God

Light: A Glimmer in the Darkness
(John 1:1-14)
    I. The Light of Christmas reminds us that God does care about you and me.
    II. The Light of Christmas reminds us that he has come to help us fight the darkness.
    III. The Light gives us hope to persevere.

Star and Stable: God's Word to Man's Need
(Matthew 2:1-2; Luke 2:12)
    I. The star and stable remind us that we need God for life and he has come.
    II. The star and stable remind us that service is the way to joy.
    III. The star and stable remind us that there is hope and help in the midst of the harsh realities of life.

The Angels: Did They Make a Mistake?
(Luke 2:8-14)
    I. Were the angels wrong? No, we were wrong for we have looked for God in the sunshine when he dwells in the darkness.
    II. Were the angels wrong? No, we've been wrong in that we've sought the wrong kind of peace.
    III. Were the angels wrong? No, we've been wrong in that we've never really tried the Christ they sang about. (This sermon idea came from Gordon Clinard.)

The Gift: The Blessedness of Receiving
(Luke 1:46-48)

I. When we receive Christ, we have our need to feel worthwhile answered.
II. When we receive Christ, our need to be needed is answered.
III. When we receive Christ, we discover help for living.

The Many Sides of Christmas

The Disturbing Side of Christmas: Fearing What Christmas Brings
(John 1:9-13)
I. We can fear Christmas because it challenges our ideas about ourselves.
II. We can fear Christmas because it challenges our concepts of faith.
III. We can fear Christmas because it challenges our ideas of Christian living.

The Love Side of Christmas: The Wonders of His Love
(Eph. 3:14-21; Luke 2)
I. The wonder of his love is that it comes to every one of us with no strings attached.
II. The wonder of his love is that it is personal.
III. The wonder of his love is that it will never stop, no matter what.

The Truth Side of Christmas: The Timeless Truths of Christmas
(Luke 2)
I. Christmas is the truth that God is actively involved in accomplishing his purposes in this world.
II. Christmas is the truth of how free we are to live responsibly for him.
III. Christmas is the truth that God has come to help us live.

The Practical Side of Christmas: Catching Christmas
(Luke 2:29-30)
I. To catch Christmas, we need to live hopefully.
II. To catch Christmas, we need to live with confidence in God's action.
III. To catch Christmas, we need to serve the Christ who came.

Christmas Is . . .

A Time for Reflection: Recapturing Our Vision
(Luke 2)

    I. We need to recapture a proper perspective about life.

    II. We need to recapture the vision of brotherhood, of concern for one another.

    III. We need to renew our commitment to discipleship to Christ.

A Time for Realism: Walking to Bethlehem

  (Luke 2)

    I. To walk to Bethlehem to worship Christ is to run the risk of pain and sorrow in order to express our love.

    II. To walk to Bethlehem to worship Christ is also to seek courage to stay in order to serve.

    III. To walk to Bethlehem to worship Christ means to have a willingness to die in order to serve Christ.

A Time for Celebration: The Active God

  (Luke 2)

    I. We can celebrate the fact that God is active in showing us he loves us dearly.

    II. We can celebrate the fact that the active God comes to us to help us live the life we ought.

    III. We can celebrate the fact that God is active and will help us to overcome our obstacles.

A Time for Receiving: Making Christmas Last

  (2 Cor. 5:16-21)

    I. We need to receive the gift of accepting love.

    II. We need to receive his gift of forgiveness.

    III. We need to receive his work and his mission.

Christmas Revelations

Christmas Paradoxes

  (Luke 2)

    I. There is the paradox between human harshness and human kindness.

    II. There is the paradox between what God is like and what people are like.

    III. There is the paradox between joy and terror.

Christmas Fear: What About It?

  (Matt. 2:1-8; Luke 2:8-20)

    I. We must discover the source of our fears.

    II. We must learn how to deal realistically with our fears.

III. Our fears can be overcome by the love of Christ.

The Real Story

(Gal. 4:4-7)

    I. The real story of Christmas is of a God who came looking for us.

    II. The real story of Christmas is that God understands what we face.

    III. The real story about Christmas is that God came seeking to redeem us.

Christmas Forgotten: After Christmas, What?

    (Matt. 2:12)

    I. After Christmas, we ought to gain a new perspective and appreciation of life and everything we do in it.

    II. After Christmas, we ought to live with a renewed confidence that God can help us face and handle the unexpected occurrences.

    III. After Christmas, we ought to have a deeper commitment to Christ.